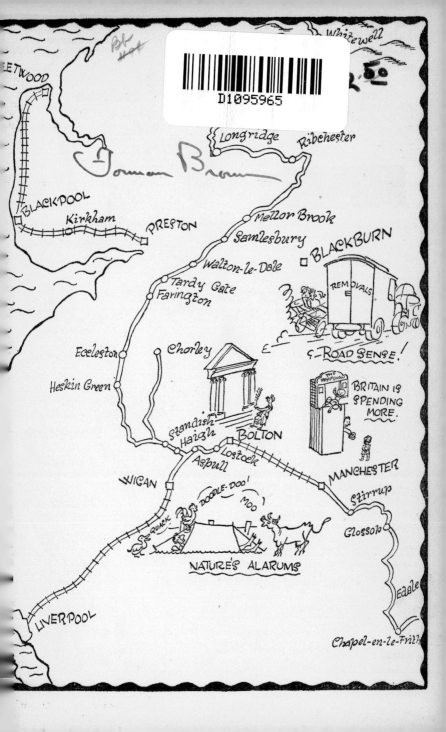

PUPPETS THROUGH LANCASHIRE

BOOKS BY WALTER WILKINSON

*

THE PEEP-SHOW

"To me a book like 'The Peep-Show' reveals England better than twenty novels written by clever young ladies and gentlemen."

D. H. LAWRENCE in *The Calendar.*

*

VAGABONDS AND PUPPETS

"Walter Wilkinson tells the story of his Puppet Show with a charm that would have delighted George Borrow himself. A book of rare fascination, romantic, picturesque, and yet entirely actual."

The Daily Telegraph.

"An endearing volume. One likes it, and one feels that one would like the author."

ARNOLD BENNET in *The Evening Standard.*

*

PUPPETS IN YORKSHIRE

J. B. PRIESTLEY wrote: —

"I was first attracted by 'Puppets in Yorkshire' because it obviously dealt with my own country; but when I came to read the book it was not the theme of Yorkshire, but Walter Wilkinson who held my attention. Walter Wilkinson is a tremendous find. England comes alive beneath the wheels of his Punch and Judy cart. I feel like rushing off to him and offering to beat the drum in front of his show."

*

A SUSSEX PEEP-SHOW

"A wholly delightful book. It is a more than worthy sequel to Walter Wilkinson's previous books, and, without the slightest imitation, a worthy successor to Hilaire Belloc's book on Sussex, 'The Four Men.'" *Manchester Guardian.*

WALTER WILKINSON

PUPPETS
THROUGH
LANCASHIRE

NEW YORK
FREDERICK A. STOKES COMPANY
PUBLISHERS

PRINTED IN GREAT BRITAIN

CONTENTS

vii

CONTENTS

I

EDALE AND SOME RAIN

SO, there I was on the road once more, pushing the camp and puppet-show before me, and under a strange oath to myself to walk with all this caboodle through the county of Lancashire, to move on from day to day, and with no more sensible object than just to see what would happen.

The immediate road was not in the least interesting and nothing at all was happening. There were new bungalows, new little villas, a sidewalk with kerbstone and lamp-posts complete, and a procession of lorries and cars coming out of Manchester. It is true that the road was a curving terrace on the hill-side, and one looked out over a wide valley to the hills of the Peak district, spacious tracts of freedom, of tender greens and greys and fading blues, swelling to the blue heavens ; but they were things apart, a world removed from this devastating company of new houses, all horrid in shape and colour, and all stuck stupidly on the edge of the road to catch every particle of dust, every concussion of sound, and every waft of the petrol exhausts.

Nothing was happening except that I was walking, and if, between you and me, reader, you have forgotten the meaning of the verb " to walk," it is this. My feet were on the ground, supporting my body, which I propelled forward by placing the left foot before the right and then the right before the left. This repeated movement of one foot before the other advances the body from one position to another and in the old days used to be known as walking. It is similar to the modern means of propulsion known as " hiking," but was not so self-conscious and affected. It is necessary to give this explanation because so many kind readers of my books will insist upon asking me what make of car I use, and do I have a trailer or a motor caravan.

I was walking, and nothing was happening, and it was impossible to imagine exactly what would happen. Every year the chances of an itinerant showman become less and less. Village greens have been converted into War Memorials, and the squares of little towns and villages have become car parks and omnibus stations, and are too noisy and too dangerous for an out-of-door artist. The traffic everywhere makes the assembling of a casual crowd increasingly difficult. At any moment, in the remotest depths of the country, a motor-cycling club might pursue its way through your crowd. A coach is always probable, and on the very evening when you decided to perform the village idiot may have just purchased a new motor-bike and is determined to show off its paces up and down the village street. And for the most part our country population now employs motor vehicles to spend its country evenings in the nearest town, or the car has made organisation so much easier that every village has its clubs, dances, theatricals, lectures, classes or whist drives arranged for every day of the week.

2

It is significant that travelling theatrical companies, cinemas and the like have gone out of business, while travelling marionettes have been off the roads these thirty years or more. The itinerant performer has been forced off the roads to the sea beaches or amusement parks, where he is no longer itinerant, but a fixed business, renting his pitch from year to year, becoming a recognised fixture and always expected to be there. The travelling showman is only an idea existing in the minds of literary intellectuals who yearn for the " Open Road." And the idea dies hard. It lives on in the cinema, in second-class literature, and in the minds of innocent romantics. It persists with me because I have tried to do it, have found it interesting, and have set up a mechanism in myself that obstinately refuses to be stopped. It is a rare person who knows when to give in, when he is beaten. The difficulties and impossibility of being a travelling showman are not my fault ; it is the fault of the whole blessed world that conspires to suppress travelling Punch-and-Judies.

Then the camping is an unknown quantity. You cannot just walk into the first delightful meadow you see. You must obtain permission from the owner. You find his house, walk across a mile of fields to find him, and then discover that he is intending to put a bull in that field and that all his other fields are occupied. You move on to the next farm and repeat the process, and you can begin asking for a camp at five o'clock and not find yourself settled until eight.

In spite of all this I walked on, determined to see what would happen. The Old Encumbrance, my

3

strange barrow loaded with puppet theatre and camp, was trundling along easily, moving smoothly over the tar between the bungalows, and I was sustained by the thought that in the evening I would be in the heart of those far-away green hills. In the meantime it was annoying that all the dogs, at the sight of the barrow, should rush to the bungalow gates and bark like demoniacs. My shoes were not down-trodden, the ends of my trousers were not ragged, and I had on a clean shirt, but the dogs did not approve of a man walking along the road. They scampered down the garden paths, bared their teeth, and accompanied my passing with fiendish growlings and barkings. Dear little " Spot " was frantic with rage and ferocity ; darling little " Wimsey " was a fiend incarnate, and ducky wucky tiddlums Mummy's little darling " Boy-Boy " was on his hind legs, yapping, snapping, and whining through all the interstices of his gate in turn.

The behaviour of the human beings was quite the reverse. The paraffin lady, a camper herself, was envious ; the baker said, " And very nice, too ; " the fruiterer thought it an excellent way of seeing the country, but the grocer, who peeped at me over the tins in his window, was a little enigmatic. He left his shop and dashed across the road with apron flying to find out what I was all about. He placed me to his satisfaction.

" Theer wur a man in my shop t'other day as said 'e couldn't stay anyweer. Spends a summer on one coast, and the next on another. Works for a week or two for

4

a farmer and then goes on. When 'e came into my shop 'e 'ad just 'ad four days in mill, but after four days 'e 'ad come out in horror, 'e said. Couldn't stand the feeling of being imprisoned, 'e said. Ee! theer's some foony folk abaht an' all, theer is! Well, I hope you 'ave a good trip."

I " tripped " on without getting any nearer to those distant hills, but turning down to Chinley I was able to sprawl out on the grass by the canal side and initiate the free and roving life with a varied lunch from the bags collected in Disley and Whaley Bridge. Chiefly, I remember a large bunch of young carrots. The shop-woman had said, " They are very expensive," and magnificently I had taken the whole bunch just to show that I was above such considerations. It was three weeks before I saw the last of those carrots. I nibbled some that day, new little carrots, very juicy and re-freshing, and excellent food, but this was the first day of vagabonding, and to be eating raw carrots as one sat in a field was a trifle alarming.

As a matter of fact I was in a very bad temper. May had been a fine, ideal camping month, but circum-stances had kept me indoors, and I was now starting off with a suspicion that the English summer was already over. And I was tired with a winter of hard work. At the first little hill on the road the barrow had seemed an enormous weight, and myself as weak as water. Panting and struggling, I hated the barrow, and loathed the towering lorries that rolled by so easily. The drivers grinned and lolled in their padded seats ; all the dogs barked ; I realised that I was not

B   5

so young as I used to be, and what with one thing and another I was in a real bad temper.

What was I doing ? There was no need to push this eccentric barrow about in search of pennies ; a couple of respectable engagements would furnish more money than I would be likely to collect in the streets through the summer. And was I going to write another book ? I had already written five books on the same theme without meeting with disaster, but to turn out a sixth was a simple invitation to have the thing flung at my head. Was I to go on for ever grinding out *Pups in This ! Pups into That ! Pups through the Other !* I was sick of puppets and puppet-showing, and of being entertaining, and I wanted to settle down into being an irascible old man and enjoy life for a bit.

It was just before Chinley station that a very sharp hill finished me off for the day. I turned into the station and within ten minutes a train was taking me through the tunnel under the long, long hill that leads into the valley of Edale ; for with the characteristic illogicality of the human animal I was starting my journey through Lancashire by going into Derbyshire.

The evening was calm and fine at Edale, and the ten minutes' train journey had completely restored my equanimity. I trundled the barrow over the short grass of two or three fields, crossed a couple of rugged brooks, and set up the tent in a high meadow, some hundreds of feet above sea-level, over the three farms at Ollerbrook. Behind the tent was a sheltering line of trees, and on all sides rose the Pennine Hills above the valley. The field itself roughened off to the tough fibres growing among rocks, and then to the rocks alone, rising to the very edge of the tableland of the Peak. It was a magnificent setting, the very place for camping. The tent went up with complete satisfaction, and after making my first soup I struggled into the sleeping-bag and, lying out like a great green caterpillar, closed my eyes.

But not to sleep. A sense of chill was dominant, and I got up to close the tent a little more, and to add a jacket to the bed-clothes. A light puff of wind went through the trees and the tent rattled lazily. Still I did not sleep, and rose again to put on a pair of socks to induce that sense of slumbrous warmth. More puffs of wind joined together into a decided breeze, and I closed the tent but for a small crack.

The breeze became a wind and the tent sprang into life, billowing, crackling, rumbling, joining with the wind in its frolic. Draughts came under the tent from every direction, icy draughts that became colder and more noticeable as the wind freshened. I got out of the sleeping-bag again and put on a woollen jumper, but then my legs were cold and it was not long before I added trousers to my night attire, and put a mackintosh over the bed as well. The final effort was to heat some water and to tie it tightly into a glass bottle ; with the help of this I did sleep fitfully until the wind became a gale, and at three o'clock I was wide awake watching the tent sway this way and that, in an attempt to pull up the pegs and snap the guy-lines.

For the rest of the night, and all next day, I suffered

7

the north east wind that tore down the valley, and for the second night I wore two of everything, was loaned a real hot-water bottle and an extra shawl, and was able to sleep the cold hours away, awaking on the Saturday morning completely refreshed and entirely acclimatised. The wind was still blowing, and bringing floods of rain with it, but the human body has wonderful powers of adaptation, and to be inside the tent was to feel flushed, warm, and comfortable.

Down below in the valley was a half-circle of bell-tents where the unemployed clubs of south-east Lancashire and north-east Cheshire were also initiating the season's camping. For nine shillings a week an unemployed bachelor could have a camping holiday there ; a married man paid seven shillings and sixpence, and in both cases the club funds contributed to make up the difference in the total cost. They had a house to fall back on with a dining-room and a club-room, but the first nights in the tents seem to have been similar to mine. There had been a good deal of getting up during the night to arrange and rearrange beds in order to avoid the rain and the veering wind.

The puppets were to perform in the evening to the campers, or rather to a combined audience of camp, village, and countryside, because it seemed a good thing that the unemployed should enjoy the luxury of giving a party, and be included in the normal run of life as much as possible. The travelling butcher had been asked to spread the invitations on his rounds, and I wondered how he had managed the matter. If he had known that the showman was a vegetarian he might not have been very pleased with his mission. It was an awkward job, anyway, as a puppet-show means nothing to most people, and I should think still less to the inhabitants of the remote Edale. My imagination was obsessed with something like this :

Enter BUTCHER (*sharpening a knife*).

BUTCHER : Loverly meat ! Buybuybuybuybuybuy !

FARM-WIFE : Have you a nice piece of mutton ?

BUTCHER (*clutching a gory chunk of fore-leg*) : Mutton ! Lord love you, lady ! Loverly mutton ! Beautiful mutton ! Have you heard the news ?

FARM-WIFE : I'll take a bit. What news ?

BUTCHER : That'll be one-and-ten. Why, there's going to be something on at the camp to-night.

FARM-WIFE : Hum ! Haven't you a little bit more fat ? And what are they doing now at the camp ?

BUTCHER : There you are ! Full weight ! Why, there's going to be something daft—a pooppet show or something, they say.

FARM-WIFE : A pooppy show ? What ! Pooppies ?

BUTCHER : No ! I've got some fresh sausages— marionettes, like. Anybody can go. I'm going. Well, you see, I serve 'em with meat. (*Bashfully.*)

FARM-WIFE : They've been to me for eggs. How much is it ?

BUTCHER : Nothing to pay. 'Tis a gentleman from London, they say, doing it. Just a party, like.

FARM-WIFE : Then happen I'll get along.

BUTCHER : Thank you ! Good day, mum ! Nice piece of liver for Thursday.

The flapping camp marquee, not quite erected, was not inviting on the wet and windy evening, and it was decided to hold the performance in the house, which, incidentally, the group of camp workers had just beautifully decorated. The warden produced a couple of lamps, the crafts instructor with three-ply and tables contrived magnificent reflectors, and the show was set up in the dining-room. With a dozen people and a chair or two the room was full ; with an audience of sixty or seventy it was practically filled to capacity, and if we campers had had a cold time we were to make up for it now.

These mixed audiences of town and country can be difficult sometimes ; neither side will give the game away, and unless the country sees that the town is laughing they are not amused. And if the country is amused the town will turn supercilious. But this was a delightful audience. I liked it, particularly the farmer's wife in a pink velvet dress—with lace. It put up one of the best performances I have ever known on the part of an audience. The travelling butcher must have done his job well after all. It laughed and clapped, and one small voice said after every scene, " And what comes next, I wonder ? " It is the sort of unconscious remark that makes a showman interested in starting a new scene. Some of the unemployed clubs have been producing puppet-shows, so the campers were prepared for the performance, but the valley folk were rather puzzled, and exclaimed, " Why, it looks like a Poonch and Joody show ! " as if it were a little below their dignity ; but I was relieved to hear one of them say later on, during the performance, " Eh, but it's beautiful, isn't it ? " in low and reverent tones.

That was good enough for me, and I could go back to the tent and freeze cheerfully after such an unsolicited testimonial. We all came out of that hot little room into a cool and clear moonlight, some to walk across the fields to farms, others to the village, and I to climb the hill back to the tent. On the way I was well filled with hot milk, and with another hot-water bottle I walked across the meadows with no fears for this night above the valley that was so still in the moonlight and so serene after a rackety performance.

The pitch in Edale was so perfect in its setting of the famous Derbyshire hills that it seemed foolish to move away too quickly, and I decided to stay over the week-end before going on into Lancashire. It was certainly a beautiful pitch ; I could realise that, but my nerves were so played out after a hard winter of performing that I could not react with the usual sympathy to that fine landscape. I expected to, but failed. For once in my life I was in the position of those awful and terrifying people who say, " I can't see anything in the country." I could see nothing in it ; it was all very dull, and monotonous, and deserted, and it would have been necessary to brighten those hills a good deal before they could have moved my moribund emotions. They needed syncopating, or " jazzing up," or treatment by a Movement for a Brighter Countryside if they were to attract any interest or admiration from my stupid and jaded sensibilities. It seemed that some rest and recuperation was necessary, and I sat in the tent the best part of the next day, sewing patches on the fly-sheet.

It was Whitsuntide, and pedestrians were streaming over the hills and down the valley all through the fine holiday. One party wandered past the tent, but, finding their way up the hill obstructed by a stone wall, they came back to ask if there was a gate. I conducted them to the projecting stone which serves as a stile and said that was the way over. But they did not think much of it. It was not their idea of a stile at all, and wasn't there some way round, like ? I left them sitting down to consider it, and forgot them.

But I was reminded of them the following day. It seems that they had funked the simple stile, and after pulling out the loose stones from a sheep creep had crawled through the hole and gone on their way rejoicing without replacing the stones. Consequently, sixty sheep, equally rejoiced, had walked through also, deserting the tough herbage of the fells for the new meadow-grass. And now it was going to be impossible to keep the sheep to the fells. After tasting the new grass nothing would keep them from it. They would leap the walls, or knock them over under a mad, ravenous desire for better food. It was going to mean a lot of work for the farmer and a harassing time for the sheep, but the miserable wretches who could not get over a stone wall would still walk the world unreproved. If this should meet their eye I hope they will have the decency to kick themselves. Country Life should become a subject in every urban school, and it should be explained that the country is rather more than just a lot of dirt, and that without the careful work of farmers all town life, all city pomps and nonsenses, would look extremely foolish.

My word! We were angry! And after that all the rain was blown back, and Edale was a dreadful hole in the hills filled with driving rain, wandering mists, and fierce winds for two days and nights.

II

BY THE PEAK AND MORE RAIN

THE morning was showery, but under the influence
of a cheerful cuckoo and some larks and thrushes,
that had been completely silent for two days, I packed
up the barrow, shoved it over the wet fields, and,
joined by an escort of three friends, moved off to get
out of the valley by way of Mam Tor, a stiff mile of
hill leading to Rushup Edge and the road to Chapel-
en-le-Frith.

As we crawled slowly up the pass all that wonderful
country was revealed, and we looked down into the
valley and across to Nether Tor, Upper Tor, the
plateau of the Peak, and all the great hills thrusting
up into the grey sky, with bright green foregrounds
before us, and a shining wet valley beyond. The view
was magnificent, as was the rain ; it swept over the
valley below us, and over the peaks above us in grey
blocks, and streamed down our beings into our boots,
but it did not stop the comic cavalcade of dripping
figures and puppet barrow from arriving at the summit,
a most satisfactory pass, a perfect V shape, with the
edge of the road at the bottom and nothing but sky
beyond—a gate into the next world. Thanks to the
good help of my friends, and with their blessings, I
went on down the other side, a dripping figure of fun.

It is curious that with all this uncomfortable weather my health was rapidly improving, and after walking a little without rain, and changing from a cold, dripping condition to being warmly damp, I began to see Derbyshire instead of pneumonia and chronic rheumatism. And I sat very cheerfully under a tight, windblown thorn bush when it rained again, and actually enjoyed a scratch lunch mingled a little with the raindrops. I enjoyed it. I did not care if it did rain—not much—it only seemed the natural conditions for that hilly part of the world, and I could have cried exultingly with the peewits that circled over the fields, because a little buoyancy was creeping into my spirits.

When the rain slacked off from the deluge to a mere steady downpour I emerged from the thorn bush, and was soon thoroughly wet again, and when you are so wet that you cannot get any wetter there is nothing more to worry about—you just slop along and curse everything and think how nice it will be when the rain ceases. The downpour changed to a driving mist, and it was not bad walking along that road. I could see a large piece of Derbyshire, several hills, a village, some farms, and a vast acreage of the rain-grey country that was not at all dreary, being shot with strange lights so that a field here stood out marvellously green, the valley there was glowing with silver light, then a ghostly patch of sunlight wandered across the fields, and suddenly the rain had ceased and the grey film had lifted from the vast scene.

With a dripping hat on one post of the show, and

an equally dripping " mac " on the other post, I progressed like an old-clothes shop, but began to dry out and to feel less cynical. With the cessation of rain a number of characteristic phenomena appeared over the countryside. The road was like one of those advertisements that want to sell a railway ticket, a packet of chocolate, or some foot powder to " hikers." The fields are tip-tilted just as they are in the posters, and you look down the chimneys and into the neat yards of the grey-stone farms below the road. Through a gate in a stone wall emerges a youth, bare-kneed and bare-headed, who crosses the road and disappears through another gate to follow that high path on Rushup Edge to Edale. A tandem pushes up the hill propelled by a young couple in velveteen shorts and bright yellow, sleeveless shirts. Three pedestrians with mountaineering boots and huge rucksacks troop by. Then it is three untidy lads, with battered old bikes rattling and clanking with ill-concealed camping equipment scattered all over them—sooty billies, chipped enamel mugs, and a scrambled up tent. We all smile at each other nervously and venomously, all having hoped to get the countryside to ourselves.

The hat dried, the " mac " dried, the road was downhill, the road-workers roared out a hearty " Ah d'ye do," as if you were a mile away, and naturally my thoughts turned to the idea of giving a performance in Chapel-en-le-Frith. As I came into the little town the rain came too, and I turned off into the Hayfield road deciding that a camp would be more appropriate than a performance. And I was right ; it was a foul

16

evening, and I did not get the chance of seeing if Chapel lived up to its distinguished name.

Bole Hill—that is the name of it—and Bole Hill together with the rain finished me off for the day. The hill was steep and all the world was blotted out with the downpour, but at the summit, out of this mad torrent of water, there stared at me a notice, POTS OF TEA. This was none of your timid offers of tea, a cup of tea, or tea with cake, this said POTS, and the gargantuan invitation appealed to me at the moment. Pots and pots, and yet more pots, I thought, and was soon sitting before a red fire burning in a large range, while the woman made an enormous kettle boil. She produced some salad and eggs, and some currant pasty, and a meat pie which I turned down.

" Well, it's not oop to mooch," she said. " Ah put it in oven before it was properly hot, laike, and it 'asn't coom aht raight, y'see. Well, you can't do everything, and me 'oosband's gone to market and left me with t house, and the feeding. And then there's the milking. Ah suppose 'e doosn't care who does the milking s'long as 'e goes to market. Well, it's an ahting, laike, and 'e'll be cooming back droonk abaht seven. And it doosn't matter what ah say abaht it. 'E'll 'ave forgotten everything by the morning—what 'e's said himself, and what anybody's said."

A dog leapt into my lap, and five tiny chicks before the fire chirruped incessantly. A young girl entered the room, home from the mill it appeared, and covered with snow-flakes, which turned out to be cotton wool, the industry of the mill. Mother and daughter started

17

in on the flat meat pies, while the daughter told a thrill-
ing tale of a girl of fourteen who had left work at five
o'clock yesterday, and had not been seen since.

" Girls of fourteen are silly," said the mother.

A wandering look came into the girl's eye, and she
said :

" She might have been knocked down by a car and
taken to a hospital."

" If she'd gone straight home from her work she
wouldn't be missing," replied the mother.

" She may have done," replied the daughter, " but
she had to get home ! It may have happened on the
way—anyway, I'm not fourteen ! "

" No, but you can be as silly," said the ingenious
mother.

I began to admire the dog in the hope that this
battle of wits would not develop, and I learnt that the
dog had been brought home by the master on one of
his market evenings. In the morning the little dog
was a stranger to him. He had forgotten entirely how
he had acquired it, but retained a story that it was
worth three guineas and that it had been ruined by
over-feeding.

" Ee ! 'E'll be cooming in droonk soon," continued the mother, " and ah don't know 'ow 'e'll be.
Are you going to camp to-night ? It looks more laike
camping indoors, ah should think."

The rain was lashing against this house on the hill-
top, and I agreed, but she could not let me have a
room as it was Whit week, and the house was full of
lodgers.

" But you could camp in our field at back, if you laike."

So, before the irresponsible husband came in I retired to the field " at back." It was a camel's hump of a field, and not before I had climbed to the highest, the windiest, and rainiest part of the meadow could I find a place for the camp. I set my teeth, and put up the tent on what was little better than the top of a sponge under a shower-bath. But when I had been inside for about ten minutes, and the stove was roaring, I was wonderfully comfortable; it was difficult to imagine that I was sitting in a damp, wind-tossed rag of a tent on a bleak hill-top intersected by grim stone walls, and surrounded by deep valleys hidden under an appalling mist of torrential rain.

III

BRIGHT PERIODS
MODERATING TO SQUALLS

HAD it still been wet in the morning I might have sold out and taken to selling umbrellas for a living, but the sky opened up very reluctantly and a little sun struggled through to the damp earth. There is hardly any pleasure in the world to compare with a fine morning after three days and nights of camping in the rain. You know then what the sun means to the world, and spreading out the blankets, sleeping-bag, clothes, and shoes on the stone wall became a religious rite. An absurd lark joined in the thanksgiving. He was sitting on the wall, singing as he sat, an unusual sight to me, but why trouble to fly when he must have had all the sensations of being in the sky. We were at the top of the hill, the stone wall curved over the crest like a vertebra, and we looked down perpendicularly on the roofs of the farms in the valley.

It was midday before the camp was thoroughly dry and packed, and the day's journey started by lowering the barrow down the meadow, which was like the side of a house. On the road to Hayfield was every kind of wheeled vehicle, a fidgety road, and when I was not tugging up a stiff hill I was resting among all the exhortations to drink pots of tea, minerals, beer, and

" New Milk Daily," which set me wondering how else it could be new. Numbers of camps were in the bottoms by the stream under Chinley Churn, and all the happy campers were spreading blankets and making their toilets in the sun.

It was still Whit week and a great many people were out to see the country. I walked with a loving couple before me, in brilliant costumes and berets, who hugged and kissed as they walked, and was followed by a family party with a perambulator. Every bank supported resting cyclists ; cars had drawn into niches, while a procession of coaches, buses, and cars ground their brakes and roared their accelerators as they all tried to pass each other. My private opinion that it was all damned awful is unmentionable, so let us concentrate on the scenery, which, I suppose, was quite good, but there was no time to observe it.

Coming into Hayfield I nearly pushed the barrow into a young woman who stepped out into the road without warning to " snap " the young man sitting on the wall. In avoiding her I forced a car to swerve rather suddenly, and I found that I did not like being a pedestrian with a barrow on a popular road. It was not pleasant at all. And Hayfield, with its meeting of roads was no place for an impromptu performance. The policeman was amused by my passage, for which he held up the traffic, and asked cheerfully if my licence was in order, and why was I not marked " Learner." But it was not pleasant on the busy road, and soon after Hayfield I tumbled into a meadow and hid behind a wall for a couple of hours, quite sulky that

C   21

so many people should want to travel the road I was going. I did not enjoy it at all.

And then in the afternoon, which was hot, you might have seen me continuing and suffering purgatory on that hill from where you take the entrancing footpath to Kinder Scout. I would have liked to walk that footpath winding over the bilberries, and along the wood, and out to the heights, but instead I toiled painfully up the road under a bungalow where the proprietor stood and stolidly watched my slow approach and the struggle past his house, and when I turned round a few minutes afterwards he was still watching. I was not enjoying this at all, but it suddenly occurred to me that the country was getting very distinguished and that at the top of the hill I was likely to be rewarded. I got to the top, literally threw the barrow to the wayside, and climbed with relief to a perch among the heather and the bilberries.

I sat there for a long time in the sun with the hills of the Peak rising in blues and browns and greens from the green trees in the spreading valleys, while overhead you could hear the small, sweet song of the high larks. The sun was warm, the air was soft, and I sat in that immense, colourful, and musical serenity suspended in a Nirvana of loveliness. It was surprising how quiet and removed the hill-top was from the wicked road only about twenty yards below. A constant stream of those curious little things—what do you call them ?— invented a few years ago—those mechanical little beetles —ah, motor cars, that's it—a constant stream flew over the road, but not one paused at this grand and exciting

22

climax of the hill between Hayfield and Glossop. Even the cyclists walked to the brow from one side to the other, and then immediately mounted to rush down the other side. Two motor cyclists had flung themselves down under a wall from where they could see nothing, and only a family party, who looked like mill-workers, were doing the right thing, that is the adults were sprawling in the heather and the children were running about prettily, picking flowers. But when a cow put her head over the wall and lowed gently the children shrieked, " A coo ! A coo ! " and rushed back to their elders.

I was torn between camping on the hill-top and in going down into Glossop to try and get some pennies for a show. I had to be in Manchester on the Monday and I had a faint ambition to walk there, which would mean pushing on farther this Friday evening. So, like a fool, I took the road again, and went down steeply towards Glossop with a new range of hills and valleys extending far and wide before me.

The chosen road skirted Glossop, and I walked on through an area of small cottages. There were very few people about, but after being emboldened by tea in a " pub " I stopped at one of the gaps in between the blocks of cottages where some children were playing, and, with a beating heart, asked a man if he thought I might give a performance there. As a matter of fact my question was an announcement that I was going to give a performance and that I hoped he would look at it and make the nucleus of an audience.

" What is't ? A Poonch and Joody ? " he sang. " Ay, ye' might get a few rahnd, laike," and the mean

23

fellow, who had been standing there very comfortably until I arrived, turned his back and disappeared into one of the houses. It was not very encouraging, but by this time the children had taken possession and I was determined to experiment, and I put up the show with its back to the communal closets, with gaily striped doors like bathing machines, and its face to the street. The children danced and pushed and slapped each other with excitement, and shouted to some others. I suggested that they should run off and collect some more audience while I prepared the theatre, but they were too afraid of missing the performance to leave me. They only insisted that I should begin quickly. They wanted to see it. They behaved in the way I would like to behave at some of these plays where the intervals are longer than the acts.

I dashed through a scene or two hoping that the noise would attract a crowd, but as only two men appeared on the other side of the road I held up the show for a bit to give the news a chance to spread. Then I started again. I could not spare much time as I had yet to find a camp for the night. It was fine, but it would take time to clear the houses, and I thought all this out as I went on with the show. The children laughed and shouted, and tried to grasp Punch's legs as they dangled over the platform. In fact, they made so much clatter that the performance was mostly a matter of the puppets trying to make the audience keep quiet.

" Now then ! Keep quiet ! I want to sleep ! " cried Punch lying out on the shelf. Immediately enormous shouts arose from the children.

" Wake oop, Poonch ! Wake oop ! Hi ! Hi !
Poonch, wake oop ! "

There was the ominous crack of a stone on the
proscenium and Punch awoke with alacrity, appealed
for order, which he got at last by making more noise
than the audience. He had very little idea of what to
do now that order was obtained, but John Barleycorn
foolishly cried to the children, " You can't do this," and
brought his head with a terrific crash on the side of the
theatre. The audience went to pieces at once and
responded with an indescribable clamour. By this time
a few adults had joined the children and by degrees
some sort of a performance got into swing. I brought
it to a close and dashed out with the hat. There was a
slow and reluctant dipping of hands into tight pockets.
There was the clip-clop, clip-clop of clogs going off
suddenly down the street.

" Nay, Ah've got nowt for yer," laughed a large
woman, and so unashamedly that I am sure she spoke
the truth.

" Wheer d'ye coom from ? " asked another woman.
" You don't belong to these parts, do you ? "

" An' can yer maike a livin' at it ? " demanded
another.

These questions received only very brief answers as
the children had gone to the back of the theatre and
were all poking their heads under the curtains. One
boy had a puppet in either hand and was cracking their
heads together, making them carry on a polite conversation in a fierce, guttural voice.

" Ah d'ye do, mister ? "

" Ah'm all reaght, Mr. Poonch ! "

" Are yer ? "

" Yes, Ah'm all reaght, Poonch."

" Are yer ! Then take that, then ! " and bang ! went the heads together as if they were as strong as the finest steel. All the children wanted to follow suit and had to be forcibly restrained. It was no easy job to pack up in the middle of that excitable swarm, but the barrow was ready at last, and I marched on to find a camp, eightpence ha'penny the richer for a very uncomfortable hour.

The cottages and houses continued and I feared that the road was only taking me deeper and deeper into the wide spreading tentacles of Manchester. After some time I came into the Hollingworth road, which was roaring with traffic, and all confusion with huge lorries piled with towering loads, with cars and cyclists. The prospect of a camp was no nearer. Through the gaps in the houses there were occasional tantalising glimpses of Chinley Churn and Abbots Chair rising serene and holy in the evening sun. But they were far away and apparently the nearest possibility of camping. If I just went on, following the main road, the only prospect was to camp in Piccadilly, Manchester, for the night.

" Are yer camping, laike ? " The unconsciously ironical question came from a curious man at a corner. He gave me advice, and pointed the way. " But ye'll 'ave a tidy broo ter get oop ! " he added, by which I imagined that I was in for a good hill. I panted up the long gradient with a walking cyclist, and he also gave me advice, directing me to a regular camping-ground down by the river at Broadbottom.

26

It seemed a long way, and the sun went down. I went up hills and down hills and through two distinct villages joined together by the interminable houses. At the very end of all patience I broke through the habitations at last and descended a steep hill under trees to the river at Broadbottom. The glimpse of a tent through the trees was encouraging, but when I got a full sight of the terrain it was to see a small paddock packed tight with cheap tents, and not the least room for one more. Seeking farther I came to another paddock, an exposed, threadbare piece at a corner, over-looked by a row of cottages. That was equally packed, and a quantity of dishevelled lads and girls were washing, playing accordions, and pushing each other about. It was a chilling sight for an enthusiastic camper like myself to see so much camping, and as the river beyond was attractive, and there was a farm showing among the trees, I trudged on, nose in air, in the hopes of getting quietly and decently settled. But the farm did not encourage camping. They had had too much trouble already from the congested camps, which, they said, the police had found necessary to visit from time to time. They advised a farm on the hill across the river that took campers. I might get in there.

A damp air was rising from the low, river fields, and I was exhausted. A bridge conducted me across the wild and picturesque River Etheron, and a quarter of a mile of footpath brought me to a stile, an awkward obstacle for the barrow. And over the stile was the path up the hill, a series of footholds on rocks, knobs of earth, and tree roots up an almost perpendicular cliff, an even more formidable obstacle than the stile. Some passers-by were willing to help, and recommended me to the owner of the fields by the river. I climbed the cliff and sought him out, but he was unwilling and suggested the farmer up the lane.

The farmer up the lane was a man. I explained my predicament and the difficulty of getting the barrow over the stile and up the cliff.

" Well, I reckon we two could get it up, couldn't we ? " and without more ado we went down to the barrow reposing behind the stile. I took it to pieces, and, one by one, we shouldered the puppet box, the camping box, the theatre, the kit bags and finally the truck itself up that cliff. We were like brigands conveying treasure to a remote cavern concealed in the high woods. It was a scene from some schoolboy adventure book come true. The earth was treacherous, and an unguarded stream fell in a waterfall to one side —a dark, deep, rocky ravine. At the top we forded the stream, scrambled up a farther bank, and deposited the pieces at the foot of a meadow inclining steeply to the darkening sky. It was an unbelievably wild corner to be so near Hollingworth and all that industrialised area. It was a return to nature with a vengeance. Having reached the bottom of the meadow, it was necessary to reassemble the baggage on the barrow and then to haul it up that slippery green slope. Halfway up there was an awkward kink in the ground, and, as we were both out of breath, both streaming with perspiration, both gasping like rusty bellows, we halted.

" Look here," said the farmer, " ah'll show you

something ! " and he led me over the grass to an open pit shaft.

" Joost look down theer ! Did you ever see owt laike it ? Ah've covered it time after time with wood, and iron, and only last week ah brought down a piece of corrugated iron and laid it across. But it's only followed all the rest of it—all gone down the bottom. Ah've informed the police, and they've looked at it and ordered the tenant to close it in. But nothing's done, and theer it is ready for any child that laikes to roon into it—or anybody. It's downright murder. Well, ah've done all ah'm going to do—ah can't do more. What d'ye think o' that ? "

In the darkening evening, with my legs shaking, the black, gaping hole was terrifying, and will haunt me for many a day. I will always be searching the morning paper, now, for one of those tragic little paragraphs : " Two boys, playing in a field on Stirrup Edge, yesterday fell into a disused pit shaft, etc.," and I wish it was covered up, and wonder how many more old pit shafts are lurking in the long grass.

We returned to the barrow, and at ten-thirty it was deposited in the farmer's field with congratulations and relief all round, until I remembered that I had pitched my hat off and left it down below. It was eleven-thirty before the tent was set, and it was twelve-thirty before I collapsed into the sleeping-bag, for I had to drink a glass of milk with the farmer in his kitchen.

I was half asleep before the sleeping-bag received my aching limbs, but I was soon fully awake, listening to three youths who had suddenly arrived at a tent a few yards away. The tent was about two feet high, and I could not sleep for trying to imagine how the three of them could get into it. It must have been one o'clock when they began to make tea with great hilarity and immense volubility. The conversation proceeded through a series of mock quarrels :

" Yer ain't lit the primus properly ! "

" Yers ah 'ave. It'll burn blue in er minute ! "

" Yer poomped it too soon ! "

" Naw ah didn't. Ah poomped it proper ! "

" Yer poomped it too soon. Ah saw yer ! "

" Wheer's the tea ? "

" You 'ad it ! "

" Naw ah didn't. 'Arry 'ad it ! "

" 'Arry ! Wheer is 'e ? Theer 'e is ! 'Arry ! Wheer's the blinkin' tea ? "

" You got it ! "

" Naw, ah ain't."

" Yers y'ave, yer silly gawp. Ah saw yer put it in t'bag."

" 'Ere it is, 'ere. 'Oo put it theer ? " and so on interminably with thick, coarse voices that growled out horrible snatches of songs, luscious growlings about love.

Fortunately I fell asleep, but on waking at five o'clock the trio were still as hilarious.

" Get oop a bit, can't yer, 'Arry ! Yer pushin' me aht of the blinkin' tent ! "

" Get oop yerself ! It's your kipper feet—yer ought ter leave them ahtside the tent ! "

The bickering continued for an hour, and then I

slept again, but was soon awakened by the united guffaws of all three, who then, apparently, dressed, and washed themselves in a small stone trough which they called the old Roman coffin a great number of times. They then retired to a chicken-hut immediately behind my tent, and while one practised haltingly on a very loud accordion the others beat out the time with their feet on the wooden floor. When there was a semblance of melody they roared out something about " Sails in the sunset," or " The music goes round and round," but the accompanist always got lost when they sang, and the singing trailed off into louder stamps and hoots of laughter.

Meanwhile I lay prone, exhausted by yesterday's efforts, too feeble to object or join in or to do anything but stagger through some breakfast and read a newspaper that I had already read. A strong, cold wind was blowing a hissing mizzle of rain on the tent, and there was little invitation to go outside. I was perfectly content to sit, enclosed by the few feet of air space and the couple of yards of ground-sheet, and let the world go by. But I wished it could have done it a little less noisily.

The farmer came at length to see if I was alive. He had not seen me stirring and he was alarmed, imagining that perhaps the evening's performance had been too much for me.

" You do see such things nowadays of people going off sudden, just dropping down, like, and I thought, maybe, it had just been too much for you, getting up the hill last night."

If I had been finished off it was consoling to think that this kind and considerate host would have done his best to give me a decent funeral.

He sat in the tent and entertained me with tales of horror. Where the tent was pitched had once been a row of houses. The whole hill-side had been covered with small holdings and his barn was made from two converted cottages. The hill had been prosperous, but now all that had vanished. Down in the valley were the mills that no longer made the world's cotton. I had passed one—an enormous structure rearing itself out of its supporting cottages, a monstrous box of window after window, surmounted by a hopeless-looking sign, TO LET OR TO SELL. And who or what, I wondered, could ever buy such a thing.

" Theer are hundreds down theer wi' nowt to do. It's awful," he said. " Every man ought to have enough work at least to keep him alive. But theer's nowt for them to do. Hundreds of them ! And now they tramp up this hill craving for work—craving for it. And ah know what that means—ah was out myself for two years."

He recited the story of his life, of having started as a boy and finishing up in the analysts' department with responsible work at a good salary.

" Then came the slump and I had to go. The manager buried his head in his arms when he told me, but I had to go. They'd kept me on for weeks doing nothing until I was ashamed. Then for two years I was looking for another place, but ah couldn't get in any-wheer—and it wasn't for want of trying. So I bought

32

this farm. I didn't mean to stay ; I thought I might make something of it and then pass it on. I don't like it. You're not your own master nowadays, farming. The Government makes you do this and do that, and not do the other, until you don't know wheer you are. Nearly killed myself last winter. I had beasts every-wheer ; in that barn, pigs over theer, cows, a bull— everything full up. And they want looking after like a lot of kids. They get sick, won't eat, and go sulky. I did have a winter of it—never again."

We were imprisoned in our tents on the hill-top most of the day by the rain. The mist cut us off from the rest of the world, and the lads from Manchester sat about in their small tents, cooking or washing-up whenever I saw them. All but the immediately ad-jacent three, who retired frequently to the chicken-hut and practised again and again on the infernal accordion. It was the farmer's injunction that they were not to be rowdy and that they must only use the instrument for playing tunes. The tunes, as far as I could disentangle them, numbered three, but there was a lot of ground to get over before the air emerged—shakily—and then the voices always joined in to drown it.

It was not till the Sunday that the landscape opened up, and I found myself perched up over a world of hills and valleys. Somewhere down there was the tragedy of cotton, miles and miles of it, but all that I could see was a summer landscape with a soft hint here and there of a chimney or a block of houses. At the bottom of the valley the River Etheron, with no fish in its industrialised waters, scrambled through the river meadows and under the trees, and on the opposite hill-side reposed the farms, quietly persisting through the rise and fall of the gigantic industry that encroached upon their ancient fields. But behind the hill lay all Manchester, and I prepared to move on into the city.

IV

MANCHESTER FORGETS RAIN
FOR ONCE

AS I came into Manchester all the respectable
people seemed to be leaving the city. A long
stream of city folk were hurrying, on either pavement,
towards the station and, could it be that they were
running ? The impression was of flight, as if all these
respectable men in neat lounge suits, on that fine evening, after performing dark deeds of business in all those
solid Victorian buildings, were all in flight, either in
horror at the deeds they had done, or because of the
attraction of some brighter life. Scurrying along the
avenues of brown bricks, skipping over kerbstones,
leaping before vehicles, the strong pushing by the
weak, all Manchester seemed to be escaping from
something, hurrying to those brighter suburbs where,
the bricks are red and the gardens green.

But I could see on coming into Piccadilly that this
flying army was a mere handful, and that a far bigger
press of people was thronging the pavement, looking
for the evening's amusement in the cinemas and restau-
rants, a throng surging this way and that on the pavement between the flower sellers in the gutter and the
bright shop windows. It was a relief to find that the
city was not emptying into the country as I came in

from the hills and that the streets were bustling with a bright, animated crowd that evidently meant to stay in those busy, spacious, but well-packed ways.

Turning from the stream into the narrower channels between the endless blocks of business houses, I came into Great Ancoats Street, where there seemed to be less bright paint and plate glass and more of the dusky brickwork, and as I proceeded the paint became decidedly old and cracked, and every shop appeared to be a second-hand dealer's—all enshrouded in a dusky brown-ness. There was no bright shopping crowd here and no flight to the station. Life was more normal, with a wild woman or two in shawls carrying small parcels of shopping ; a faded old man gnawed a dirty, unfilled pipe at a corner ; a party of factory girls were walking home, or some shabby children were bouncing balls, talking and moving in an erratic, jerky way, doing their best to get under the trams which rolled by, bright, majestic chariots in this dun world. It was all a disgrace to the fine May evening, and I began to envy those in flight to the station.

Before a dark and sinister railway bridge I turned off into Every Street, to be confronted with a long, double row of little houses running over a curve and dwindling in the distance to the foot of a very tall and forbidding gasometer. Again it was all the dirty grey-brown, not actually a colour at all, but a fusty channel of dirty bricks and pavement, with the dim gasometer brooding at the end of it all and lending a slight tinge of gas to the fusty air.

There was an odd look about the houses that rose

36

straight from the narrow pavement; under each one was a half-buried shop, as if the whole street had suffered a landslide and was living in the ruins. And yet the arrangement was intentional, as some steps led down to the submerged half of the shop below the pavement, but it affected me unpleasantly when I remembered myself, as a small boy, peering down into just such a cellar shop trying to discover in the dim interior a tailor who had cut his throat the night before. These little buried shops are made more melancholy by being closed, shuttered, and barred nowadays, except for one in which a cobbler still works with his head on a level with the pedestrians' feet on the pavement.

In between each of these shops is a flight of four or five steps to the front door of the elevated cottage, and these steps are the one charming note in this ditch of brickbats, for they are all whitened and ochred and gleam forth from the dun surroundings, bright symbols of man's—or woman's—eternal effort and aspiration to make the best of a bad job. It leads one to suppose that the interiors are equally well cared for as far as the resources of the family will go, but there was a grimy, gritty feeling about it all that already made me long for a bath and a change of clothing.

Withal, the inhabitants appeared to be very much alive. Men and women were sitting on the clean steps, leaning against doorposts, and standing at open doors, engaged in animated conversations, while the children dashed about the pavement, shouted about nothing, swung on lamp-posts and bounced balls, while one group was playing at school with a yellow varnished school-desk and seat set out on the narrow pavement. It was in this Hogarthian scene that I had wanted to set up the Peep Show and give some performances—I cannot say why—except that it would have been a dramatic contrast to my winter efforts in the city, when a politer Manchester had given the puppets so kind a reception at the University and the luncheon club. The authorities, however, had forbidden such a proceeding, for they had visualised the Peep Show acting as a sort of Pied Piper, attracting a following of children that would inevitably become entangled with the traffic. They could not allow any fun in the streets ; they were reserved for traffic, which, of course, is anything but funny nowadays.

Luckily in Every Street there is another symbol, besides the bright streets, of man's attempt to stem the tide of business beastliness. The Manchester University has long since established a Settlement in the Round House there, an old Swedenborgian church, and where the Swedenborgians used to amuse themselves by singing hymns, Mr. and Mrs. Rendel Wyatt, with a group of cheerful workers, now perform good deeds by organising classes, lectures, unemployed clubs, benefits, dances, and anything that will give battle to this depressing area, this dirty legacy from those virtuous Victorians, that now, in the face of the public opinion of the good Manchester people, is to be razed to the ground.

The Round House has been beautifully decorated by unemployed members of the Settlement—none of them professional decorators—but the work is well done, and testifies to their willingness to work if only some amiable exploiter will come along and try to make a bit out of their labour.   But they wait and wait, grow soft, develop a nervous, not-wanted sort of manner, cadge cigarettes from daughters in work, settle down into a placid, drifty way of life or—commit suicide.   And it was here, at what is called an " At Home " evening, the puppets were to perform to an audience drawn from the district.

As I set up the theatre members of the club swept the floor and arranged the chairs.   Two of them approached the stage piano and one of them began to play while the other sat down to admire him.   The pianist went on and on, from one tune to another, never at a loss for a note, pouring out a flood of overbearing sound that filled the hall.

In an attempt to get some rest from it I offered the pianist a cigarette, and asked if he had learnt all that by ear.   He nodded dissent to the first and assent to the second, but he did not cease playing.   He nodded, fell out of time for a moment, and then came down heavily on the loud pedal, and floated out again on the ever-flowing river of sound, the interminable flood of melodies that were all different and yet seemed to be all the same. It seemed a marvellous talent to me, to be able to make so bold with such a formidable instrument as the pianoforte, and yet it was hardly like music.   As he played more men gathered round, and broke out into frightful choruses—"The skies are blue, I'm waiting for you," but it seems that they were on forbidden ground,

A caretaker suddenly turned them all off and they went mutely, but I did not like to see those grown men being turned off like small boys. I wished that they had shouted, and damned the regulations, and gone on playing and singing—if not quite like men—at least as brave and courageous beings.

The audience began to take its seats very early ; the local population, it seems, likes to come and just sit in the Round House, and be expectant, I suppose. A number of old ladies were there, and a good few old gentlemen, dressed in their ancient best. There were also some children, and, more particularly, some of the actors of the unemployed dramatic club. This company had just produced *Julius Cæsar*, and, by special request, the puppets were to perform the " Quarrel Scene " from that play—with Brutus sitting in the front row.

From various accounts I gathered that this production of Shakespeare's play had been of a lively nature. The actors are very vigorous, especially in the fighting scenes, and owing to a slight accident during rehearsal with a metal dagger the lady responsible for the production had procured some ingenious weapons made of rubber. When the rubber daggers flopped about like so many herrings, and finally when, with an extra thrust at Cæsar, one of them curled up, the audience was hilarious, and the children had become so out of hand that a vow had been registered never to admit children again. But they had come in to the puppets, and behaved in an exemplary manner, laughing at all the right places, which shows that they had good manners and were well versed in the art of pleasing a

40

showman. As for the actors, they gave a warm reception to Cassius and Brutus, and Brutus himself, in the front row, was " laughing like old anything."

Life in the Round House goes on. There is so much that can be done that life has no beginning and no end for the wardens, and I packed up the show while a band assembled to play for a " sixpenny hop." In the wings I was apprehensive as brilliant saxophones were put together, and a flashing and terrible array of drums, cymbals, and Chinese gongs was set up, and it is true that when the whole lot was let loose in the not very full hall it was exceedingly difficult to concentrate on what I was doing. The beats of the leading pianist shook me like an earthquake ; the drums went on and on and on, in the maddening barbaric way these drums do, and the saxophone, that unsteady, imperfect, and disgusting instrument in the hands of a vigorous un-musician, reduced my packing to the utmost disorder. The couples seemed to like it. They danced sedately, and sat out the intervals sedately and correctly. If you are a product of an intense industrial district I suppose this kind of music is sweet and tender, but I had come in from the decent country, and it all sounded like rusty railway trains gone mad. I retired to my bedroom in the Settlement and looked out of the window into the garden to soothe my fretted nerves. Five cats were prowling round the meagre bushes that the Settlement had planted there, and one wondered whether it was kindness to the neighbourhood to attempt a garden, or cruelty to the plants.

Sleep mercifully intervened to prevent me thinking

at all seriously about the life around, but I was awake sufficiently early to hear the " tapper " going up the street waking the clients by rattling on their bedroom window panes—a time-honoured custom that must be a bit expensive nowadays. You pay, I believe, a penny a week for having the life frightened out of you by window panes rattling in the eerie dawn ; a half-crown alarum-clock would be quite as terrifying and uncomfortable, and you would have some pennies left over to buy a consoling cigarette or two.

V

BOLTON RAINS PENNIES

FROM Manchester I tramped on to Bolton—by
train—but had to manœuvre the barrow across the
city to the station. I did not relish the job, but
fortunately I fell in behind a lorry drawn by a horse,
and was able to maintain a slow, cowardly, but comfortable progress through the traffic. When I realised
that it was a railway lorry, and that it would shelter me
all the way to the station, a prayer of thankfulness went
up to the patron saint of travellers.

And I did not relish going to Bolton. I had been
there once in the winter on a dreadful day of smoky
rain, and I had thought Bolton to be the most awful
human settlement it was possible to be in. But this
day was clear and the sun shining, and I soon began
to think that it was one of the pleasantest towns to be
in. It is not too big and not too small. It has not been
wealthy enough to erect enormous and hideous buildings,
but sufficiently rich to house its industries neatly and
without ostentation. The streets are wide, and every
few yards there is a delightfully painted and decorated
little shrine fixed to lamp-posts. They are designed
with such care and artistry that some religious significance was suggested, but I discovered that they were

43

for litter, and raked my pockets for suitable donations to as many as possible.

The puppets had come into Bolton because the clever and thoughtful educational authorities are studying the use of puppet-shows in the schools. It was at first thought to be a frivolous suggestion, but now that the movement has swept through all British schools, they seem to have been fully justified. It is a belated attempt to adjust the one-sided nature of education that has tended to deprive children of playing imaginative games or of amusing themselves in any original way whatever. As regards the educational value of puppet theatres there is a strong case. In the first place, the making of a theatre employs a good many useful crafts. Carpentry is brought in with the construction of the theatre, and if it is anything like the carpentry we used to indulge in at school a good many planes will be wrecked and some curious theatres evolved. Some sort of modelling or carving will be necessary for the heads ; the costumes will provide a varied experience in needlework, and, the costumes being small, the experience will be gained without a vast expenditure of time, money, or material —although in my case a good deal of patience was expended. Girls, of course, used to get this practice in dressing dolls, but nowadays, even if little girls condescend to dolls, they most likely select the dresses from a catalogue of ready-mades—at bargain prices— telephone the order and pay by cheque. There is then the question of a performance, the scenes to be selected or invented, and finally the actual presentation, which will exercise the speech and singing of the manipulators.

44

Incidentally, it is an all-round introduction to theatre work, and as a great many children will be employed in theatrical productions, and as all of them will help to make audiences, and their criticisms or likes and dislikes will influence the quality, it is as well that they should have some conscious and educated knowledge of what it is all about. On top of all this it is an exhilarating and interesting incentive to children to develop the imaginative and inventive sides of their minds, and anything that will do that for children ought to be encouraged. At all events the schools that have made themselves puppet theatres have found the children to be keenly interested and amused, which is sufficient justification as far as I am concerned. It would be delightful if some school would write its history in puppets, make caricatures of the Head, the staff and the pupils, and contemporary modes and theories of education ; and if succeeding generations continued to add to it, why, what a puppet show that would be in a hundred years time !

So it had been arranged that I should give five performances in Bolton schools to help on the good work. A schedule was given to me and a plan of the city, which all looked very simple, and I set out for the first performance, allowing an hour to push the barrow there and to set up the theatre. But it was soon obvious that Bolton, as a city, is much too large, and after half an hour I was still a long way from the school and still toiling up the eternal gradient of Chorley Old Road against a strong head wind. Panting, and quite dizzy with seeing so much of Bolton, I arrived at the school with ten minutes in which to find my way into the far-flung building and prepare the theatre. But that was only the beginning of a fierce crescendo through the afternoon.

In the dash round the school—in quite the wrong direction—I was surprised to see an idyllic scene of lawns about the bright building, and numbers of girls in gay clothing sitting and playing in the grass. This was a shock, and not my idea at all of an elementary school in an industrial town. Lancashire must be clearing up the mess, and making up for the dirty old times, I thought, as I lugged the barrow up to a door and began loosening straps. Five precious minutes were lost in finding the mistress, when I should have inquired for the head master of the boys' side. Then four or five boys seized parts of the theatre and we charged into the school, helter-skelter, with long poles catching in doors and loose pieces clattering to the ground. The boys lost their way in this palatial edifice and we had to return, disturbing a girls' gymnastic class, filing perilously round the side of a swimming-bath—a swimming-bath ! Yes ! A swimming-bath, and finally, at the exact hour at which the performance should have started, arrived on the platform with the theatre scattered about in resemblance of a smashed up chicken-hut.

Pity the poor puppet showman ! Hauling the barrow up Chorley Old Road against wind and time and under a hot sun was equal to running a mile race, and now there was the scramble of erecting the theatre and the immediate plunge into a performance which has achieved a character that must be maintained, and which was to be an example to the children. And all the time I was thinking of the next performance, which was to begin the minute this one was finished, and with no time left for transferring the show to the girls' side.

But every one was very kind, and those two performances were given, and tea, even, drunk in between, but not the slightest impression of them remains to me— only the heated, breathless scramble, which culminated in a harassed lorry driver hurrying me still farther, as he had been deputed to take me to the Lostock Open Air School, and had yet to milk his cows ! But I drew the line at being the slave of cows, and dragged the driver off to a class-room of the school where the boys had made and erected a puppet theatre, and we watched two or three amusing scenes given with surprising energy and skill. It was evident that the puppet theatre will release or organise some of the immense energy of children.

At last I was driven to the Lostock Open Air School, which lies on the western outskirts of Bolton and looks over miles of lovely country to Rivington Pike, rising clear above the fields. And here, on a secluded lawn in the gardens, I was invited to pitch the tent, with high hedges to shelter me, borders of flowers laid out decoratively in the name of the school, to cheer me, and the persons of the bailiff and the engineer to entertain me.

The super-activities of the next day began with the engineer waking me at six o'clock so that I could swim in the school swimming-bath, and immediately after breakfast they continued. Making prudent inquiries, I had discovered that I was to perform at a school three miles away at ten o'clock, but the school kindly deputed Jimmy to help shove the barrow. Evidently it was not exactly a kindness to Jimmy. After all, he is a respectable citizen of Bolton, and it is no light matter to be asked to push a strange-looking barrow through your native streets. There was a good deal of banter, and a threat to fix a large L on his back. In good time we started. Jimmy had short, but very quick legs, and he started off at a furious pace that nothing would stop. Any hints as to taking it easy were only answered by lugubrious information that it was a goodish bit to go, and there was a stiff " broo " to get up. Uphill, downhill, or on the level, nothing would stop the regular twinkle of my companion's legs, and we stormed through the leafy and beautiful and extensive suburbs of Bolton as if we were escaping the police. This house was where the brewer lived ; at this mansion the chairman lived ; on that court somebody played tennis for a fee of I don't know how many hundreds of pounds. Here a winner of the Irish sweepstake had built a house, and a very fine, modern, architected stone house it was too, with a great view over the hills that lie about Bolton, and eventually we reached the school with only fifteen minutes to set up the theatre. Again, the rush through two performances, the second being upstairs, and with a door so narrow that the theatre had to be unscrewed and reassembled before the waiting audience. And finally the rush to the waiting lorry.

After lunch there was a performance for the Open
Air School, on a green lawn, of course, and after that an
inspection of this remarkable school, this brave attempt to keep the children of Bolton in good health.
Here are sent, from all the elementary schools in the
city, those children that are suffering from the lack of
fresh air and good food. They are housed and dressed
and fed and educated, and stay about a year. There is
a farm attached which supplies a lot of the food and all
the milk, and all the milk for the rest of the schools in
the city. And it is proper milk, such as few city folk
taste nowadays.

If I were put there for treatment I would not want
to go away, but could take my meals in that orderly
and spotlessly clean dining-room, and be weighed and
put on weight day by day with pleasure. Then there
is the swimming-bath, and the playing-fields, and the
class-rooms built with two glass sides that can be thrown
open to all the summer airs that warm the hill of
Lostock. And the scout room has been beautifully
fresco'd by two art students who were formerly at the
school itself.

And finally there is the dormitory. During the
evening a whistle had been blown sharply at fairly
frequent intervals, which, I learned, was to silence the
boys in their beds. The evening was warm and light,
and they were not sleepy. The matron asked if I
would like to go up and speak to them—it would be
good for them if I were to speak to them. Knowing
what boys are, I was exceedingly dubious as to any
speaking having a good effect on them, but I went up

49

to see them all in their beds, all the windows wide open, and the green trees rustling gently outside in the garden. As to speaking to them, the rascals were so suspiciously quiet that I wanted to bound round the room on all fours and squawk like a cat to give them an outlet for the energy being suppressed at our entrance. But the matron was there, and all we boys had to behave ourselves under that benign but strong influence.

Yes, poor Lancashire has been heavily weighted with the horrible industrialism of the Victorians, but the spirit of reform persists, accepts its blows, but goes on clearing up the mess.

And in the heart of the town itself they are cleansing and scouring, and round the Town Hall has arisen a crescent of public buildings, a handsome pile of stone in the classic manner. I am not sufficiently learned to say from which period it derives, whether Doric or Roman or Renaissance, but it is handsome enough to send all the citizens of Bolton into togas and into talking cinquecento Italian.

If architects are allowed to draw upon the past for their designs, it is obvious that tailors should be encouraged to do the same in search of handsome styles. It is an eyesore to see the anachronism of lounge suits entering the classic portals of Bolton's public buildings. It is sacrilege, and I ask the tailors of the city to rise up and protest against this infamy. If the Mayor and Corporation and all the Town Council were dressed in the flowing robes of Greece or Rome, or both, what a splendid accompaniment it would be to the new buildings. It would be interesting and instructive, too, and I, for one, would watch them go about Deansgate and Oxford Street with the greatest interest and admiration. If all the citizens adopted such becoming garments it would not be a wild prophecy to say that the city would have a good chance of becoming very famous, and would benefit itself by the attraction of a good deal of tourist traffic. Imagine the effect upon the envious inhabitants of the neighbouring towns :

" Are t'going to Blackpool for t'holiday, lad ? "

" Nay, ah like something a bit more amusing. Ah'm taking the missis to Bolton ! "

And if the togas were cut generously from that famous Bolton sheeting, which I hope is manufactured in Bolton and not in Wigan or somewhere—if they were cut very generously, why, all the cotton mills of Lancashire would soon be spinning again. But this serious and eminently sensible suggestion will not be adopted. It is awful to think how conservative the people of Lancashire are, and but for this slight and frivolous prejudice against wearing handsome clothes the whole county might again be prosperous. If they can work in Grecian temples, what is to prevent them from walking in Roman togas ?

VI

WIGAN BELIES ITS REPUTATION

THE famous town of Wigan being so near, it would have been a lifelong regret not to have seen it, and as Winifred was joining the expedition we had arranged to meet there. It was a very warm afternoon when I set the barrow in that direction ; it was a bright day, and the outskirts of Bolton and the surrounding hills were very attractive as I left them. Now, I was afraid of becoming involved in streams of traffic, or miles of depressing mills, or in awful areas of coal mines, but with commendable bravery I marched towards a long vague line of tall chimneys and queer-shaped erections, a long weird line in the distance that melted away into the horizon as if it were the edge of the world.

Almost immediately I became surrounded by cottages—old cottages without gardens and new cottages with gardens. Heads and shoulders appeared over walls and stared long and fixedly at me. Witty remarks were bandied from neighbour to neighbour over rickety garden fences, and an extraordinary old man, without a hair on his head and with no teeth in his mouth, but a very strong dialect, stumbled out of a cottage and mumbled a flood of unintelligible remarks within two inches of my face. Ensued a very one-sided conversation, and a long tale from him of what the doctor said about Lostock, but all I could understand was :

" Tha's wha t'docther said, but, mind you, ah doan't say tas tis."

And from those cottages I came to more, and to trams, and to high walls about large mills, with tall chimneys rising to the sky, and clumsy, fantastic, and complicated erections with mysterious functions. All the ground was packed with buildings of strictly practical designs and set at odd, incomprehensibe angles, and it was surprising how few people were about. I walked alone among all this human achievement until I was astounded to see two men squatting on the kerb at one of the corners. They squatted calmly, like Indian fakirs, but why on the kerbstone, which was only an inch high, did not seem very clear. They seemed very small and very odd with nothing to lean their backs against, and stuck out there on a corner, down on the ground, in the hunched up squat. I nodded, and mumbled a " how do," but the searching expression of the two faces was fixed, and as I passed the four eyes moved slowly across their sockets from left to right. There was no change of expression, and no acknowledgment, either in amity or mockery.

I hardly knew what to make of it, but pushed the barrow on somewhat nervously. There seemed to be some vague, inimical influence in the air. A few more pedestrians passed quietly and sedately and, even if they troubled to stare, that was all. Even the houses and the " works " with their respectability and

F

righteous industry seemed to draw themselves up in disapproval.

Presently there were more shops and more people, but the sense of isolation only increased. A group of men at a complicated corner watched me curve round to a side road, and, as I hesitated, suddenly asked where I wanted to go. As I replied they dropped into nonchalance again, and simply nodded in the desired direction. I passed on through more cottages and more indifferent passers-by, but after a quarter of a mile one of the men who had been standing at the corner with a bicycle suddenly drew up to my side and inquired if I was quite satisfied that this was the right road. We discussed the routes to Wigan, and he approved of my choice, which he agreed would be quieter and more likely to produce a camp. And it all felt more alien than ever, in spite of the considerate attention ; the sense of walking through somebody else's world and of being a strange object in need of help and guidance only increased.

It was strange how few people were in sight for so many houses, and all the afternoon I propelled the vehicle by walls, where, I suppose, hundreds of people were at work—and so very silently. Now and again I passed another squatting man, or two men, squatting at incongruous corners. Two men are walking towards me, and suddenly, for no apparent reason and with no arrangement, they suddenly fall into the squat at any old place. Occasionally a figure is seated on a chair in some door. Higher up, through Wingates, groups were sitting on a ragged grass bank over a ditch on the

54

opposite side of the road to their row of cottages, but when I came into Aspull and filed between the houses rising from the narrow pavement there was an epidemic of squatting.

As I approached, men standing in doorways and on the pavement were observable. At the first house a nose and an eye peered round the lintel watching my approach. Just before I drew level he dropped into the squat, the better to observe. It was a sort of signal. Men standing on the pavement slipped into a doorway and squatted ; men already standing in doorways squatted ; those already squatting adjusted their position a little, poising themselves, as it were, into the proper and exact squat for observing this strange thing.

If there had been any possible place to put up the theatre they would have had a full exposition, but all this part was the ribbon development of Victorian times, a straggled out district without beginning or end to the stranger, and with no possible show-ground. Those cottages had risen from the pavement leaving no free spaces, built, I suppose, in the time before it was realised that all the industrial expansion was going to cut off a whole race from the lovely and natural environment of man. So I passed on between the squatting men, squatting in the doorways of their little houses.

It is a queer world on the top of Aspull Moor, where one looks down over Wigan and the surrounding—I almost said country—but it is a country bristling with the upright chimneys ; large chimneys near at hand, smaller chimneys down in the valleys, and still smaller

chimneys far away on the distant hills. Among the
chimneys rise odd-shaped blocks, clumsy, top-heavy
towers, ugly ramifications of perched-up sheds, descending pipes, truck-tippers, elevators, inexplicable
masses of stark utility that shame the loveliness of
earth and beggar the wonderful imagination of man.
Over it all hovers an air that is not clear or invisible,
and clouds that should be grey are orange tinted ;
sunlight, that should flash and quiver on bright
colours, is a tangible film over the anæmic trees and
sparse grass. There was little sign of a camp in this
" civilised " country, and I was tired of walking, walking through village after village that made of the whole
district one scattered built-up area. Some men, sitting
under a Great War memorial, suggested farther on.
Gravely and courteously they explained the way where
a quiet farm would be found. It would have been
possible to camp there, on Aspull Moor ; the grassy
tracts between the cottages was all free ground, but
they agreed that it would not be quiet or restful to
camp in so public a place. There were no jocular
remarks, no facetiousness, not a smile among them.
They seemed to me depressed and saddened men, and
I was coming to the conclusion that at last I had come
upon a real dour race of beings.

Their mood was understandable later on when I had
passed through Haigh and did at last find a pitch. The
farm had no room ; the fields were down for hay and
the pastures full of stock. " What about over the
hedge ? " The farmer tossed his head towards a tract
of tumbled ground, littered with broken concrete and

56

odd pieces of splintered wood, rusting iron and rotting canvas. " It's an old pit—no one would object to you going there if it's just for the night."

That seemed to me to explain the repressed atmosphere of the district. Five such coal-pits had been closed down in the last few years and one-third of the population was unemployed. It may have been my own mood—my energy was certainly reduced by the three performances the day before—but it is seldom possible to push the eccentric barrow through inhabited areas without meeting with ribaldry, without demands for a performance, or without seriously interested questions as to what I was doing. It is true that, later on, the people of Haigh did very kindly ask for a performance ; but actually, as I first passed through the village, they had taken me for a travelling draper—a more sensible conclusion than ordinary. But Haigh is a distinguished village. Its eighteenth-century-looking cottages climb a hill, high above all the Wigan district ; it has a good old inn, and it had an ancient hall. Its inhabitants must be descended from the earliest coal miners, and they are strong in race.

So, appropriately, I set up the tent on the ruins of the old coal-pit and shut myself up to myself. Some youths whistled affectionately from the railway bridge, but I was cooking, and was too deeply immersed in the difficulties of *Tschiffely's Ride* to be drawn.

It was necessary to get a good pitch this day, as Winifred was coming into camp—and she was coming from Paris—and I could not see a traveller from Paris settling down with equanimity to camp on a derelict coal-pit. Something better than hot and dusty Paris, a verdant, retired and wholly delectable rural pitch must be found, something with pleasant turf and small flowers, handsome trees and a wide view, but where, in the vicinity of Wigan, this was to be found seemed a problem as I steered the barrow over the lumps of concrete, the rotting boards, and mouldy canvas to the road.

Near the gate something was bobbing about among the stones, and going over to see what it was, I discovered a man's head sticking out of the earth. Into a sack he was pitching tiny pieces of coal that he was grubbing from the hole in which he stood. And what a tragic tale he had to tell! Out of work, of course, and here he had been slaving for a week to get a heap of coal out of the old pit. He had arranged for a pal to meet him this morning, and between them they were to have shouldered the coal to the village. But, when he arrived, his precious hoard of coal had been lifted; the pal had got in before him, and he was left to start the miserable scratching in the hole again. I proffered a cigarette by way of consolation, and he jumped out of the cavern to tell me the wretched tale all over again with added adjectives and gusto.

This was no help in finding a delectable pitch, and I walked on disturbed, for the unemployment question starts my mind off like a sky-rocket to discuss our social organisation, or rather to howl it. What if the man's coal had been taken? A mean trick, of course. But I expect he was the stronger and ready to fight for it, which is exactly what happens at the back of all employment. All competitive business is developed on warfare—the potential power of being able to knock your opponent on the head, and it is either just as mean or just as noble as the coal pincher's little scoop. It is small beer to worry about the morality of unfortunate people on the dole. That is not where the trouble lies. It is in the dangerous immorality of people off the dole —a long way off !

There was a lot more of it, but I was suddenly pulled up by a flash of bright colour—a red admiral butterfly settling on a large leaf. As I stopped to look at this un-Wigan like phenomenon I became aware of birds singing, too, and emerging still farther from the brain storm it was to realise that here was a country lane and fields over the hedges, bright green fields, and hawthorn bushes cascading white blossoms among the greenery. I might have been almost anywhere in England. It was a winding country lane, winding among quiet fields, with graceful trees decorated with singing birds, and Wigan—that butt of every comedian —was barely three miles away. The delectable camp did not seem so impossible after all, and, continuing, the lane carried me over the placid waters of a canal, by some cottages, and across a main road where, once more, were the tall chimneys, the overhead wheels of a pit, and a large works. But the lane continued across the road, by a small whitewashed cottage, and then under old handsome trees with a large and ancient farm behind the trees. Some inquiries and a good deal of waiting at last deposited me on the edge of an uncut hayfield, where I put up the tent, looking out to a pleasant enough vista of meadows and trees. It was almost the perfect pitch. The trees were large and lazy ; in the distance rose an ancient church tower, and only here and there among the trees a distant chimney disturbed the rural scene. And it was here, after an interval of bus and town, that Winifred stepped into the story from Paris—and, after five minutes in the tent, could hardly believe that she had been there at all, and even wondered if that city really existed.

VII

CAN YER MEK' IT PAY?

A VERY wet night was disturbing, but as we went into Wigan the next morning the clouds lifted, and a little sun came over the bright suburbs, the little modern villas, the gardens and the trees. It was a shock to preconceived notions to find that Wigan is a hilly town, and that streets, with names like Standishgate and Bishopsgate, run up to the high centre where stands the church dominating the whole town. The breeze blows strongly there, and you look out to a large panorama and a great sky.

It was under the walls of the church that I stopped for a moment to light a pipe, but the petrol lighter did a vast amount of sparking without flaming. Seeing my predicament, a man stopped and asked if I wanted a light, producing a sensible box of matches with the remark : " Ah've never thowt owt o' they things ! "

He simply took it for granted that we were strangers, and without asking obligingly told us the way about the town. We confessed that our ignorance was deplorable, and that we only knew of Wigan through the music-hall jokes.

" That wur a Wigan man as started that," he said, " an' they don't think s'mooch of 'im abaht 'ere. 'E went dahn sahth a lot ! "

To finish, we asked him point-blank what he thought of Wigan, and, hesitating a moment while he took his pipe slowly from his mouth, he said :

" Well, ah've stook it for forty years, and ah don't feel mooch like changing nah."

Undoubtedly there is the stir of life in Wigan, and through its bright and breezy streets the coal miner boldly clippety-clops in his wooden clogs, swinging along through the shopping ladies and the High School girls like a man. The dark beams and white plaster of Old England are a decorative motif for the shops ; Old England above, but plate glass and chromium steel below, and all the " latest " in the windows. And inside those cafés, that are so smart and new outside, you will find ladies indulging in the good old-fashioned Lancashire custom of meat pies for tea, followed by the nourishing Eccles cakes lavishly stuffed with about half a pound of currants—and real fruity currants, not those four or five squashed flies you can find in Eccles cakes made out of the county.

The shops are well stocked, as they well may be, for the town serves a district of a quarter of a million people, and on Saturday night progress through the streets of Wigan amounts to standing patiently until you are shoved, I understand. Shopping there is delightful after more pretentious and affected markets. You are served by human beings who are interested in what they are doing, and who take a particular interest in you as a stranger. We entered one large store to search for a few inches of black elastic. We were passed on from department to department with such easy good manners, and every one seemed so pleased to see us, that we felt we were making friends all round. They had no black elastic, but there was no unpleasantness about it. It is common nowadays for a shop assistant to snub you if you ask for a commodity they do not sell. But not in Wigan. They tell you where you can buy it.

We heard of a South African visitor who wanted some tobacco. He was particular in his tastes, and asked for several kinds to be mixed together in the hopes of obtaining a satisfactory smoke.

" I'll take four ounces and try it," he said.

" Four ounces ! " shrieked the careful girl. " You'd better take one first, and see if you like it ! "

It was the most wonderful thing the South African had ever met with, and we recommend this treatment of their victims to all students of Sales Psychology. As a representative buyer I can vouch for its effectiveness. Rather than face the disinterested, supercilious technique of some London shops I would take the train to Wigan of a Saturday night !

In roaming the streets we observed an ancient marionette hanging in an antique shop, and entered in the hopes of finding a long-sought set of old Punch and Judy figures. The marionette had belonged to one Lewis, a manipulator who had shown in those parts, but had since gone to America. There were no Punch figures, but a beautiful collection of furniture and glass and china in Mr. Harrison's shop, and above all a very handsome grandfather clock.

" I have just bought it locally," he said. " The daughter of the house was sick of the old thing knocking

63

about the house, and she made her parents sell what she called ' a blot on the landscape.' "

The afternoon finished ignominiously at the cinema. Rain drove us to shelter, but it was not at all an ordinary visit to the cinema. We could see plenty of posters, but we could not find the houses, until, following an advertisement in a back court, we mounted some unpretentious steps, and found ourselves entering by an exit to nobody's dismay, and for the payment of fourpence. Not the best cinema, we understand, but we saw an average picture, escaped the rain, and all for fourpence. And I have a feeling that that is a fair indication of the standard of prices in the county, where the same race buys that sells and will not allow any nonsense about high prices.

It was the sort of weather when play was impossible in eight county cricket matches, and had it not been for Mr. Warburton there would have been little play for us. Mr. Warburton had seen the tent and the barrow, and, being a reader of the puppet books, he had guessed who we were. I became aware of this early in the morning when the farmer's wife had appeared in the field with a copy of *Puppets into Scotland* with a request that it should be autographed ; and the owner had hospitably invited us to use him in any way we wished while camping in the district.

Consequently Mr. Warburton and his brother arrived at the farm in a car, and lifted us out of the water-bound tent to see something of the neighbourhood, and we had only progressed a few yards when we were introduced to Worthington Manor, an old grey farm-house, and a few yards farther up the road was the ancient Worthington Hall with a pretty façade of timber work. A little farther and we passed a footpath that led to a moated grange, then it was the entrance gates of Duxbury Hall, and where we had imagined gasworks and coal-pits, mills and foundries, were grey old houses, shaky with time and history, still standing in the ancient fields.

" Those are the first houses of Chorley village," said our driver.

" It's a village, is it ? Then there are no industries at Chorley ! "

" Well, there's a few works about."

By this time we were in the " village," had rolled past a quarter of a mile of houses, the huge works of the Leyland Motors, traversed a busy side street thick with shops, and were turning into a lengthy High Street, roaring with business and dominated by a formidable Town Hall. There were side streets, churches, a large market, a Technical College—in fact, all the appurtenances of a large and flourishing town.

While still wondering why it should be called a village, we drew up at a high arch and, passing through, walked into a green and lovely park, and across the grass to that aged casket of glass and stone, Astley Hall. Its frontage has almost as much glass as our modern factories, but the thousands of small square and diamond panes are held firmly, yet delicately, by the tall lines of stone work. Two huge pillars to the sides of the door support two handsome stone lions, and in one minute

65

you stand there, among the crumbling stone and the bending leads of the windows, in a miraculous survival of the Jacobean. It is beautifully done, and Chorley is to be commended for preserving this work of art in its lovely park to show all industrial Lancashire, and any industrial maniac, how graciously man might live if he would but turn his mind to the cultivation of Art and Loveliness, and away from the fanaticism of selling *things* to the whole world.

Astley Hall is now a discreet museum. It has its panelled rooms and its rather comic ceilings ; it has some cases of simple but exquisite Leeds pottery ; there are some fine pieces of furniture ; and it has its long gallery at the top of the house, one side all panelling, and the other three sides all little diamond window panes through which you look down on to the miniature lake, the lilies, and the swans, and the greensward under the trees. There is also an amazing shovel board table in the long gallery, and after counting its two dozen legs you can speculate as to how its weight and length were got into the room.

When we came out of the house a burst of sun had brought out the cricketers, and they fitted into the handsome scene like some eighteenth-century picture, the players out on the very green green, and the supporters and scorers in groups under the fine trees. The lads were not so smartly dressed as the top-hatted old players, but the play, and particularly the fielding, was very keen as befits the lads of Lancashire.

There seemed to be no end to the old manor houses, halls, granges and parks we might visit, and on the way back to the tent we turned into Duxbury Park and prowled round the gardens and the hall, that Miles Standish, who sailed in the *Mayflower*, claimed as his family seat. But he appears to have been misleading, and the present Duxbury Hall appears to be considerably more modern than the *Mayflower*. This hall and park has also been acquired by Chorley, I believe, but has not yet been prepared for use.

As a reward for their kindness we lured our hosts into the tent, and invited them to the rare pleasure of squatting on the floor for some tea, and after that, while debating the question of showing the puppets by the old cross and stocks at Standish, the rain began whispering on the tent and ended by pelting us like so many dried peas. We were consoled by the information that, being Saturday, the inhabitants of Standish would all be in Wigan.

Already weighty with the historical knowledge we had gained during the afternoon's ride, we passed the wet evening nursing that large and thorough volume, *The History of Standish*, by the Rev. Porteous. Its erudition would have passed off us like water off a good tent roof if we had not been squatting in one of the fields of the ancient Rectory Farm, and could read how, in 1779, it had been farmed by Henry Aspinal, and that its fields were all christened with such names as Stock Hey, Higher Barcroft, The Horse Pasture and Upper Ryding. If some of our impolite motorists, who ride out so bravely into the country, realised that most fields have names, like good Christians, perhaps they would not feel so free to disfigure them.

Then there is Standish Church, which we could see from the tent, with the best oak ceiling in the county ; Standish Hall was hidden among the trees over there, where the conspirators met in secret to plot against the Jacobite cause ; and Ralph Standish, who would be a little surprised by the district nowadays, was knighted in 1381 for knocking Wat Tyler, the labour leader, about. There were coal-pits about Standish in 1634, when it is recorded that three gentlemen lost their way on the moor among them, and were only saved from destruction by their horses snapping at the invisible holes ; and in the year 1718-1719 the Standish coal-pits made a profit of £62 16s. 8½d. But now they are closed, not even capable of profiting to that extent.

And now the rain came down on Standish, on its ancient houses and its new, on the fields and the old coal-pit. A low sky shut out the light and a preter-natural gloom hovered over the district. What with the weather and the closing down of coal-pits, and the depression in cotton, a mutation of life had descended on Standish and Haigh. There was a sense of it all having come to a standstill, as if it were squatting for the time being, and one wondered what would happen next to make history in the district ; would something startling come from all those depressed people living with such tenacity in the little cottages among the chimneys.

For the whole of the next day the rain came down out of the low sky, and we sat in the tent with the con-tinual patter of the drops on the thin cotton. Out-wardly the tent was a dripping rag, and we were not

surprised when the farmer looked in on us and cried,
" Ah shouldn't care for that mooch ! "

And yet we had been occupied to the exclusion of
boredom. We had " done out " the tent, cooked, read,
played games, stimulated the circulation with a standstill Red Indian dance from time to time, and eaten again,
and here it was already evening with letters still to be
written, and a hundred things to be done. We could
almost have done with another wet day.

VIII

LIVERPOOL TO PRESTON

ACT ONE

The scene is the interior of the tent. We are seated on the floor, while the rain beats down mercilessly on the roof. WINIFRED *is reading.* C'EST MOI *is studying a map. Time 9 a.m.*

C'EST MOI : I say ! Where's Liverpool ?

WINIFRED : Why, it can't be far away. It's in Lancashire, anyhow, but I always think of it as a place apart, a sort of county in itself, you know.

C'EST MOI : Yes, you're right. I'd always a suspicion that Manchester was in the county, but Liverpool—— ! You know, I never think of Liverpool as anything but a railway station, a taxi dashing through a lot of lights, and then those weird, draughty dock buildings where you always feel like a trespasser, or a piece of baggage, or an undesirable emigrant, or a political suspect, or a lost dog, or a——.

WINIFRED : Why don't we go ? It won't take very long, and we can't walk in this weather or do any shows.

C'EST MOI : Good idea ! We'll go to Liverpool.

ACT TWO

The scene is the same. Time 9 p.m.

C'EST MOI : Well ! That's that !

WINIFRED : Do you feel you know Liverpool any better now ?

C'EST MOI : Yes, I realise it's a place, but I don't think we were very clever. It's not easy to be a tourist in your own country.

WINIFRED : Yes, it would be more interesting to come into England and see it superficially, like a stranger. But didn't you feel a bit like one with those Irish voices, and the Americans and those Negroes on the landing stage, and, remember, we did buy a guide book.

C'EST MOI : That overhead railway was lucky for a wet day. Made one feel like being in New York—not that I've ever been there.

WINIFRED : I saw enough docks, and warehouses, and landing stages from it to finish me with docks for ever.

C'EST MOI : Wonderful docks !

Breathes there a man, who ever to himself hath said,
I know those thirty miles of docks from A to Z.

WINIFRED : Don't shout so loud, you'll wake the farmer ! I liked it better from the ferry. It must be fun to work in Liverpool, and go home by steamer to

71

New Brighton. I should like to live in a port. I'm English enough to get quite excited at the sight of ships, and sailors, and ropes.

C'EST MOI : Fancy old Gladstone being born in Liverpool ! I'm surprised at him, choosing a place like that.

WINIFRED : That was nice, that road with his house, and all the Georgian-looking houses. It's curious how doctors always manage to live in the nicest parts of a town. I thought we would never find that cathedral.

C'EST MOI : Of course, we could have asked the way, but you can't ask for cathedrals except in foreign countries.

WINIFRED : But you don't forget it when you have seen it—like everything else in Liverpool it must be about the biggest in the world. There's something exciting, isn't there, about building a cathedral in this century. But I must say I couldn't help thinking to myself that human beings are both the most sanguine and the most idiotic creatures ever created, for here we are building a large work of art at the same time as we are building enormous battleships for the next war that may raze all this loveliness to the ground.

C'EST MOI : Perhaps, if more people spent their time on large buildings they'd refuse to build battleships. It's a great effort—the cathedral. I liked getting on the roof. It makes a good place for a pagan to get an exhilarating view. The custodian up there had evidently had some pretty impressive experiences of thunderstorms this summer. He got quite poetic about the way the lightning flashed about him like

72

thousands of little devils, he said. It's something to have seen a cathedral being built, and remember we saw two men fixing a stained glass window that will be looked at by the strange people living in a thousand years' time—and perhaps more. We saw it being done, we shall be able to say, and by two ordinary fellows in dungarees and shirt sleeves.

WINIFRED : You didn't expect them to wear top-hats and tail-coats, did you ?

C'EST MOI : No, but one always imagines cathedrals being built by an abbot or somebody in a costume.

WINIFRED : It's hard work, being a tourist. I am sleepy.

C'EST MOI : I'm sure I'm going to dream about the great mouth of the Mersey Tunnel and that enormous black obelisk, there. It's the biggest in the world.

WINIFRED : Yes, everything seemed to be the biggest in the world according to the guide book——. The Mersey Tunnel is the largest sub-aqueous work of its kind in the world. The Landing Stage is the largest floating structure in the world. The spot cotton market, whatever that is, the largest in the world. The great arch of the cathedral is amongst the largest Gothic arches ever constructed. St. George's Hall is one of the greatest edifices in the world, and the clock on the Royal Liver Friendly Society's building is the largest in England.

C'EST MOI : Do stop—you'll give me a nightmare. D'ye think it will be raining in the morning ?

When we were awakened the next morning at six

o'clock by thunder and yet more rain, Winifred rolled over in her sleeping-bag and said, " I'm not going to play," and went to sleep again.

There was nothing else to do but sleep and eat, wash up the dishes, and eat again. Outside, the rain was so thick that visibility only extended to about a hundred yards, and it was impossible to pack and move on without getting all our effects impossibly sodden with water. Mr. Warburton had asked us to go back to Haigh and give an evening performance in the school there, but we were loath to go back on our tracks ; if we were to see anything of Lancashire we could not sit for days in one place, and before committing ourselves to this retrograde movement we waited to see if the old adage, *Rain before seven, fine before eleven*, had any truth in it.

The skies struggled to maintain the honour of the old prophets, and between succeeding showers, thunder and flashes of sun, we eventually assembled the barrow for travelling in not too damp a condition. We pushed off into more rain, and walked and sheltered our way through Standish, advancing about two miles to the hour. Then another determined downfall drove us into a " pub " in search of lunch ; but we could get nothing to eat but potato chips out of a packet. That was progress, certainly ; George Borrow could not have eaten fried potatoes out of a paper packet ; but we were living in the twentieth century, and had advanced beyond such crude tastes as home-made bread and creamy cheese. We ought to have been pleased with the March of Time, but how we longed for the bread and cheese !

" Ah think it'll take oop, likely," said the roadman, rolling his experienced eye round the heavens, and we marched on into a sudden wind that seemed to smell of the sea ; and as the Irish Sea is only a dozen flat miles or so from the Wigan district it is possible, I suppose, that we were not mistaken in that " salty smack." At all events it was a fine wind that gathered up the low sky into firm clouds, that sailed across the heavens, and we walked along, making the most of the fine hours. We had chosen a secondary road that was certainly clear of traffic, but it had an urban feeling the whole way, and we walked between scattered cottages and bungalows that gathered up into a village at Eccleston, and then spread out again sufficiently to destroy the sense of being in the country.

Eastwards we looked across a wide view, across Chorley towards Darwen and Blackburn, and in the fresh, after-the-rain light of blue-cloud-shadow and sun, this industrial Lancashire took on a surprisingly entrancing aspect. Among the settlements of industry there is always a farm or two, or some woods, and looking over a wide area it is surprising how soon the buildings lose themselves, and what you know to be colonies of gaunt mills and unromantic lines of cottages becomes a sort of ideal world ; in this vague, misty scene of mild colour and sunlight, backed by the distant Pennines, the works and mills and the many tall chimneys rose delicately out of masses of trees and fields, distant and innocent little hives of industry that added a comfortable human touch to the vast scene. There is little doubt that the farther off you are from

75

industrial areas the more enchanting and wonderful they seem, and that is why, I suppose, those industrialists who can manage it take themselves off to live at Lytham or St. Anne's on the coast, or even go so far afield as the Lake District. It must all look very lovely from there.

It was about here that Winifred went into a small shop while I stood just outside the door. The woman had seen us coming, and began to ask questions.

" Don't yer get tired, pushing that . . ." she paused for the right word, nodding out into the road.

" Barrow," said Winifred.

" Ay, a barrer, is it ? "

" No, I like it, and it's easier really to go with it than without—it pulls you along."

" Hum ! " The old lady paused, and then with another nod said, " Is yon yer 'usband ? "

" Yes."

" Hum ! " and there was another long pause.

" 'Ave yer a 'ome ? "

" Yes."

" Hum ! Been long on t'road ? "

" About eight weeks."

" Wot d'ye do at neet ? "

" Sleep in a tent."

" In this weather ? "

" Yes, the rain never comes in."

" Hum ! "

She busied about the shop, then having made up her mind, asked the question that had been on her lips, outright.

" What's yer intention, laike, if yer don't mind me asking ? "

Winifred explained that we were pushing a show about, and camping as we went, but the woman was not altogether convinced and eyed her dubiously.

" Well, ah can see fer misel' that yer summat out t'ordinary. Ah see all sorts o' folk on't road. We get all sorts 'ere, and sin this 'ere unemployment theer's never a day goes by wi'out some of 'em coming 'ere ter beg. Ah do know summat abaht folks on't road, and ah said to misel' as soon as ah saw yer, ' Naw then, theer's summat funny abaht this 'ere couple—look at their shoes ! ' "

After some further explanation the old lady was tolerably convinced that she understood us, and Winifred asked about the unemployment, if it was bad about the district.

" These 'ere poltichuns, they're a 'ole lot of rascals, that's what they are. Should laike to see some of 'em bringing their children up on t'dole, wi' means test an' all. Some o' them could do wi' a means test. They tell us in t'papers abaht t'population going dahn, but d'yer think a decent man's going ter 'ave children when theer's nowt ter bring 'em up to ! You tell old Baldwin to put that in his pipe and smoke it ! "

We began to think of getting a camp and of finding somewhere to perform, but in this curious district of neither town nor country there seemed little incentive or opportunity to indulge in either activity. There was never a space to hold a crowd, and, anyway, there was no crowd to be gathered. At any particular point we could only have drawn on the contents of a bungalow or two, a filling station and perhaps a farm. Obviously they were not expecting a travelling puppet theatre in those parts. The only people to be seen were a few passing motorists, an occasional lorry full of workmen going home, and a cyclist or two. They were all moving on, all going somewhere else, and the local population was not in sight at all, having, presumably, travelled off in some vehicle to get away from the place in which they were supposed to live. But, of course, no one lives anywhere nowadays. We are all on the road, chasing round, escaping from something which no one can quite define, or searching for something that very few people seem to find. We were looking for an audience to amuse, but it seemed that the audience had moved away in search of amusement elsewhere. A natural effect of a too mobile means of locomotion.

As for camping, a mixture of farmer and butcher let us into a hayfield, not quite a normal hayfield, for the farmer-butcher was a builder also, and a nearly completed red brick villa was sticking up brutally out of the grass. Having procured a camp from one farm, it was necessary to approach another for milk, and while the farmer's wife filled the can, I had to stand and watch the farmer eat an incredible amount of apple pastry. In the midst of this developing world of new brick, and garages, and villas with stained glass front doors, the farm kitchen alone had resisted progress. Needless to say it was the better for it ; the simple chairs and scrubbed table, the tall clock and the chest of drawers

78

were all there in decent sobriety as they must have been for his fathers.

While I had been searching for milk Winifred had remained in the tent to cook some food, and she had been startled by a voice outside suddenly demanding heartily if she were comfortable. Busy with the cooking, she had answered a few more questions of this unseen and unknown questioner, until he had demanded imperiously, " Come out, and let's have a look at you ! "

It was only the farmer to whom the field belonged, and I suppose he had every right to treat a lady who camped on his land as if she were part of the farm stock. But he was polite enough to approve of the place in which we had pitched, but then, with his eyes popping out of his head, he had fired off a series of startling questions : " And are you going to sleep in that ? And is it comfortable ? And do you push it about on that thing ? And where do you come from ? And what's your profession when you're at home, like ? And can you make a living at it ? And doesn't your husband do any work ? And have you got owt to eat ? Well, you'll be all right—there's no bad people about here, you know."

By the next evening we had struggled through more rain to the vicinity of Preston. The road produced no excitement beyond a stretch of about half a mile where we had walked without a chimney in sight, and we had suddenly realised how very pleasant it would be when we arrived at the real country beyond Preston. Approaching Leyland, the world became more lively with a quantity of tradesmen's vans, high-class bakers,

79

low class fishmongers, no class butchers and first-class drapers, and then we were in Leyland among the chimneys, and the street ringing with the clippety-clop of wooden clogs. Eventually we were camped in a small orchard with the house immediately behind us, a splendid view of a chicken run before us, and a heavy, thundery sky above us. But the farmer and his family were so polite and so kind, that we were comfortable and at our ease. " It is at your convenience," he said, and then apologised for the fact that they would be making a noise next morning at five, when they would be up for the milking. He was a gentle, shy man, with the face of a hardened criminal surmounted by a bright cretonne bonnet—a protection from the cow's hide when milking. It was comforting to be near the house. The sky looked dangerous as if it might burst out into a firework display at any moment, and we saw ourselves taking refuge with our hosts if it turned out to be a " special gala performance."

The weather was a nuisance and we played with the idea of hovering near the towns, of even lodging in a town, and attempting to get on with some puppet showing. We had even imagined Preston to be a half industrial, half market town, where it would be possible to perform in the streets, and perhaps stroll into some schools without any formidable formalities. But after half an hour's struggling in Fishergate, and an interview with the educational authorities in the depths of a gigantic Grecian temple, that idea was entirely obliterated.

Preston has no business to be so big ! It is enormous ; its streets hum with traffic ; it is a city that sends up a roar. There is a large market, very useful to shelter in from the rain, and which deals in two Lancashire specialities—good food and materials, miles of food, and acres of odd pieces of stuffs, stall after stall piled with remainders and patterns and cuttings. Tiring of the market, we moved our shelter to the Art Gallery, and there found ourselves face to face with a plaque in honour of Francis Thompson, who, to our surprise, was born in Preston. " Oh ! of course," said Winifred, and " Of course," said I, but it was news to me, anyhow.

We wandered round the old pictures, all rather out of date, and it has to be a good picture that can stand outside its contemporary fashion. Here was Lancashire heavily weighted again with the exuberance of the Victorians, with pictures of ladies made of the smoothest china, of yearning children, of dear little cats, and dogs, and donkeys, with all the oil paint sunsets and sticky landscapes, the only excellent thing about them being the varnish which had mispreserved them, and deprived contemporary artists of all that wall space. But the modern spirit is at work, and bright, new works are stealing on to those walls ; and there is an excellent propaganda room set apart for the special exhibition of one contemporary artist at a time. I have a profound pity for the directors of our provincial art galleries ; it must be uphill work getting rid of those expensive old paintings, as big as cricket pitches, of theatrical history, and subjects like Moses being found in the bulrushes. And an industrial county ought to watch its " art." When mechanical processes are perfected and common to the whole world, it is art in the end that is going to make the commodities interesting and attractive and desirable to buyers. Mere good cotton will not be enough ; it must have the subtle charm and the fascination which art alone knows how to supply, and then, only sometimes.

From art we turned to shopping in a dry spell. As in all the Lancashire towns, the shops in Preston are served by people, which is a valuable consideration to homeless wanderers who welcome any small bit of human communication. In one shop we turned down an article that did not meet with our requirements. The shopman did his best to persuade us that it did, but we knew better, and in the end he lost the battle— philosophically—remarking that it was better to lose a sale than a customer. He then proceeded to find out a little gossip about us, and began enthusiastically to discuss the beauty of England.

" Now, Devon ! That's a luvely county ! "

" Yes, and Somerset, too," we advanced.

" Ah ! Now ! Somerset ! Ee ! that's wheer that Smyth Piggot wur, wasn't it ? "

" I believe it was—it's a lovely county, quite un-spoilt."

" Ee ! The Abode o' Luve 'e called it, didn't 'e ? The Abode o' Luve, that wur it."

" Yes, a lovely county, and you get the hills and the sea as well."

" Ee ! And they do say 'e wur nothing mooch to look at,

82

an' all, but I understand the ladies used to fling theerselves upon him—simply fling theerselves. Well! I always say the ladies see farther into a thing than us men do. Ee! joost used to fling theerselves! Now I do say——"

We began to be afraid of what the old satyr would say next about the beauties of England, and we withdrew rather suddenly, to discover Booths, the ideal grocer's shop and its restaurant. You would have thought that there was already sufficient good food in Lancashire, but here were piles of all those exotic dainties, those specialities in tins and boxes that find their way to every quarter of the globe, and we burdened ourselves with a store for the camp.

We were not doing so badly in Preston, and had managed to keep out of the showers of rain with a fair amount of amusement, and now, after lunch, we set out in search of an antique dealer to see if he happened to know where all the old Punch and Judies were concealed. But on the way, to escape a sudden shower, we dashed into a cavity which turned out to be a railway station, and there before us was the magic word, BLACK-POOL! An idle question as to trains turned our heads. The ticket collector fixed us firmly with his eyes, and said sharply, " 'Oory oop! Theer's a train joost going. Get your tickets, theer, at number two, and then it's platform four, down 'ere, second stairs on your right, an' ah wish ah wur coming wi' yer!"

Confound that ticket collector! We got on to platform four as quickly as we could, and under more exhortations from porters and guards, and whistles and flags, we dashed into a carriage and were on our way to Blackpool.

83

IX

BLACKPOOL INTERLUDE

A S we took our seats a short, red-faced fellow, with staring eyes, rose from a corner and lurched to the door, hanging awkwardly over the window-sill :

" I wan' a drink o' beer," he growled at the moving platform. " S'too late," he added, and straightening himself attempted to turn and get back to his seat, where two beer bottles snuggled in the cushions. It was not until he had been handed along by the other passengers, and had sat on the bottles that he discovered this, evidently, forgotten property. He raked them out, stared at them stupidly, and then with a radiant smile, offered them round the carriage. The proffered bottles met with a stony reception from the various ladies, but to the man opposite he thrust the bottle so persistently that finally the man took it, and pushed it away out of sight.

" That's ri' ! You're a sensible fellow ! " He opened the remaining bottle, took an unsteady drink, and then smiled benignly on us all.

" 'Ave a drink ? " he said to me. " No ? You 'ave won, missis," and he waved the bottle at Winifred.

" Ee ! it's luvely to be droonk ! " he sighed. " Ee, it's grand to be droonk ! Wur you never droonk, missis ? Then you've missed the best thing in life !

84

Ee ! It's luvely. Theer's no unemployment, you know, when you're droonk. Everybody's 'appy. You're 'appy, and theer's a luvely feeling, and light— Ee ! it's luvely to be droonk ! " He sighed and made several attempts to drink while the other travellers sat primly, trying to ignore him, or looking at him disdainfully.

" I pity his head in the morning," said one of the women.

" He can't have much sense in it," said another.

" Ought not to be allowed to travel like that," said a third.

He looked at the speakers in turn with a comic grimace, and then winked at his fellowman in the opposite seat.

" 'Ere, 'ave a drink, dad ! " he invited, waving the well-sucked bottle.

" Nay, ah doan't tooch it," said the grey, upright old fellow. " Ah want to live and enjoy meself a bit longer, yet ! "

" Then you 'ave won, missis—it's luvely to be droonk ! "

" You'd better put it away," said the woman kindly, and he collapsed, a little sadly, watching us all mutely.

At Kirkham station another woman entered the carriage with a boy, when, there being only one seat, the drunken fellow insisted upon standing and giving the boy his seat. He held the bottle behind him, wiped his mouth, attempted to set his hat straight, and smiled on the boy beautifully.

" 'Ello, sonny ! Ah 'ope you're going' t'ave a good 'oliday."

The boy smiled. The man smiled.

" Ah wish si wur you're age. Bet ah'd 'ave a good 'oliday, ah would."

The two smiled lovingly.

" Bet you're goin' t'ave a good 'oliday, sonny," and they continued to smile.

" Bet you could spend sisspence, couldn't you, sonny ? " and with bigger smiles still, with clumsy fumblings and the discovery of a bottle of beer in either trouser pocket, a " sisspence " was lurched into the small boy's hand.

" You 'ave a good 'oliday. Ah bet ah would if ah wur your age. But, now look 'ere, you listen to me." The fellow attempted to lean a little nearer the boy, swayed disconcertingly, but succeeded in grasping the rack.

" You listen to me, sonny. Don't you get drinking no beer. Don't you ever do that. It's 'orrible stoof, and once yur start yur can't leave off. Don't you ever drink beer, will you ? Promise me that now, sonny, and it'll be good for you. Once you start you can't leave off. Look at me ! Ah want a drink o' beer now. And can't get one. Ah'm miserable ! " He made a suitable grimace which started the boy laughing.

" Ah wish ah could get a drink ! Rotten train ! Can't get any beer. That's it, you keep off the drink, sonny, or you'll be like me, the lowest of the low. Nobody'll 'ave a good word for you ; nobody'll trust you. Promise me you won't touch a drop, and that'll be good for you—good for you——"

86

His head suddenly drooped and his eyes closed, but he came into consciousness again with a jerk.

" Ee ! S'luvely to be droonk ! Wish ah could get properly droonk ! Seven or eight double whiskies would do the trick—be luvely. Can't afford it. Can't afford to be droonk ! Theer's a do, an' all ! 'Aven't seen my missis for eight weeks."

" Are you going to see her in that state ? " asked a woman.

" Ee ! she won't mind. She's best old woman in t'world. Ah wouldn't change 'er for anything. But ah wish ah could get droonk—properly droonk." His head dropped again, and he began to lean dangerously towards a woman's lap. She got up and urged him to sit down, but he was too stupid to understand, and had to be lowered into the corner. For a moment he gave a glassy stare at nothing, and then collapsed with a sigh, and a low, " S'luvely to be droonk. . . ."

It made us all laugh, but one of the women, a haggard old aunty in a new cheap frock, said through her smiles, " Poor fellow," and I think she voiced the genuine thought of the whole carriage. At all events they were looking after him when we left at Blackpool, and if this one disreputable character fitted in with our ready-made prejudices, the dignified behaviour of the rest of the carriage weighted the scales heavily in the opposite direction.

Little by little we advanced out of the station and crept towards the sea. The afternoon had cleared up, the sun was brilliant, and every one was out to do his duty on the five-mile promenade or the limitless sands,

Walk, walk, walk, every one was walking, thousands of figures moving this way or that in a steady, ceaseless rhythm. In a stiff mass we shuffled across the road under the shadow of the brilliant green and white trams, and came out to the promenade with the same ceaseless walking, but with a lesser density.

The wide sands were dotted with the seated and with a few ball games in progress, and far away was a thin silver line of sea with small black figures, bathing machines, and swaying boats all along its fringe. We thought we had never seen so many people, and it was obvious that one came to Blackpool, above all, for company. Of course, there is the sea, the air, and the sun, but what are these among so many !

Above us soared the Tower ; north and south was the interminable line of hotels and boarding-houses, and for the rest thousands of the most orderly, sedate, and demure holiday-makers imaginable. Blackpool was quiet ! It was almost restful ! There was plenty of it, but it was eminently respectable, and your foreign watering-places, where the wealthy mobs gather, are indescribably vulgar in comparison. Here are four lads walking in a line ; a quiet word now, a quiet word then. That is all, and they walk slowly on at the prescribed pace melting into the general mass. Here is a family party, with grandparents all complete, one imagines. They all seem to have some new clothes. The children are all new ; the ladies *may* be all new ; father has new flannels and new canvas shoes ; but grandad seems to be wearing his usual dark grey Sunday suit, with a bowler hat, and new canvas shoes only. They walk past silently, but happily, the children with rock. Now it is two very short spinsters, a young married couple next, also very small, two young girls, more lads, more family, an elderly bachelor alone, the types repeating interminably, all walking on the promenade, all in holiday mood and canvas shoes, and all in the gentle ecstasy of being in good old Blackpool once again.

" Coom 'ere, Annie, you'll get lost ! "

" Coom 'ere, muther, 'ere's Joe ! "

" Coom 'ere," said the ventriloquist, seated on top of a step-ladder. " Ah pay forty pound to the corporation for this pitch, and it's your money ah want ! " And jerking its head in the direction of two passing men, his doll squeaked, " Wheer's t'going ? S'too laate to sign on nah—coom 'ere, ah wants tha ! "

There was a policeman on the sands, but all he could find to do was to fraternise with a baby donkey. As he stood with hand extended to the infant animal one could imagine him saying, " Yes, little comrade, the law is an ass to be in such a well-behaved place as this." But it is more likely that he was saying, " Coom 'ere ! "

" Coom 'ere ! " said the children to their balls. The oyster stall said it to us, and we said it to each other. Three pretty girls acted it to three shy lads. The girls were playing with a ball—the lads watching. Presently the beautiful ball, which had been bouncing merrily, was examined closely by the girls, and under their scrutiny the ball mysteriously collapsed. The flabby object was held up in dismay. What a shame ! They could play no more ! But fortunately one of the youths reacted to this form of " Coom 'ere ! " The practical business of inflating the bladder gave him confidence. Oh ! Clever young women ! There were soon six young figures playing with the ball.

In these two words seem to lie the soul of Blackpool ; it had itself uttered the simple invitation which echoed through all the mills and cottages of Lancashire, and here they were, escaped from the looms and spindles for a brief spell, in good old Blackpool again, enjoying themselves all very much together.

If there was one thing more than another that interested us in this marvellous Fun Fair it was, naturally, the Punch and Judy shows. There could be no question of our performing in such an organised and be-rented place ; it was our turn to be one of the crowd, and we found a show in progress in one of the three booths that are established on the beach. The performance was the usual remnants of better days well enough done, with the more rare appearance of the old character, Scaramouche, who startles Punch deliciously by extending his neck to the length of some two feet, and thus enabling himself to see round the sides and over the top of his theatre.

" And how's business ? " we inquired of the showman.

" Well, we mustn't grumble, but the weather has been bad. We were two days off last week, and three days with nothing doing the week before, and a morning here and an afternoon there. The weather has been dreadful and, of course, the corporation must have their little bit whatever happens. We don't seem to get so many of the right people nowadays. I don't like to say it, but they seem more—more—well, more common, if you see what I mean. Of course some are very nice. We get some nice ladies and gentlemen, who are like me and can still enjoy the old show. It often makes me laugh now, although my father did it before me. Now last week we had a crowd of two or three hundred sitting down there in front of the show—came from Oswaldtwistle, or somewhere. But, you know, I don't believe I hardly got sixpence from the lot. I don't know how it is—times are bad, of course. There's a lot of unemployment, but it wasn't hardly that. It was more that they didn't seem to think there was anything to pay for—but, of course, they aren't all like that."

Tiring of the walking, we indulged in another of the sports. We mounted an opulent white tram, and let it carry us to Fleetwood, which, we had heard, still retained the character of an old fishing village. All the way there it seemed to be still Blackpool, more and more miles of promenade, all a little newer and brighter, not penetrating so deeply inland, and not quite so thickly populated, but still Blackpool. At Fleetwood itself there is a little comforting real life in the shape of fishing trawlers and the L.M.S. railway station, but otherwise it is all gaiety and phantasy, flower-beds and pavilions, ice cream and cafés.

It was while passing a gap in the many flowers that we caught sight of a small-sized pierrot theatre in a corner beyond the children's paddling pool. Pulled up by its diminutive appearance, we changed our course, and so discovered Mr. Bilton's Minimites or

Marionettes, about to perform the play of Dick Whittington.

Up ! went the curtain—at least it did finally with the assistance of Mr. Bilton standing on a chair—and some very bright marionettes performed an incident from the early life of London's most famous Lord Mayor. It was all considerably enhanced by the antics of Lazy Jack, the villain of the play, and, of course, the cat, that bounded as high and as enthusiastically as only marionette cats know how. Wow! and it leapt to the ceiling. Would pussy like a meal ? Wow ! and it leapt again. Then there were the sausages and the rat ; they also vied with the cat in leaping to the skies. It was quite the children's idea of dramatic movement—and mine, too !

Mr. and Mrs. Bilton's marionette theatre is a charming addition to the childrens' playground, and they have a delightful way of fraternising with their audiences. Mr. Bilton is a musician, the harp his instrument, and the next time we go to Fleetwood we are promised some harp music as well as the marionettes. All honour to this artistic corner of Fleetwood, which is far better for the children than the eternal ice cream and toffee, and is more likely to awaken their minds and make men and women of them.

But that was not the end of puppet shows ; we were in for an orgy of the art, and a little farther on we came to the Punch and Judy of Mr. Carcass. Mr. Carcass is in the Italian tradition, his ancestry being Neapolitan. His great-great-grandfather was in the profession, his grandfather, seventy-four years of age, is still performing at Brighton, and his daughter, aged eleven months, was sitting there, learning the job from her father. He handles his puppets with assurance, and his Toby is a deft assistant. His Punch is a joyous fellow who chuckles continually, and in all his slap-stick Mr. Carcass contrives a spirited rhythm. It was interesting to see one of the figures lift a hand and remove its hat, a trick which I have never seen before, but which is mentioned in that Covent Garden show, which Cruick-shank portrayed, as being the trick which had lifted this particular showman above his rivals.

The night came down on Blackpool, and the lights came out, and under the electric signs the crowds continued to walk, walk, walk. The circus was full, the cinemas were full, the dancing-rooms were full, the amusement park was full, the bars and cafés were full, and in the Tower the lift-light continued to go up and down, up and down, in and out of the dark sky. I suppose an upbringing in a cotton mill or a coal-pit is necessary to allow one to realise the real charm of Blackpool. It is all very well done, but we turned to the tent and a quiet corner in a field, with the feeling of returning to real life again out of a suffocating jam of too much of everything.

X

MORE RAIN THAN BLACKBURN

WE were pushing the barrow again, circling round Preston to get into the famous Ribble Valley. After a mile or so of town streets, and directions from a polite householder, who raised his hat to Winifred, we emerged into a forgotten lane and, once past an enormous gasometer, we were astonished to see over the hedges and hayfields a strange, romantic city rising delicately in the misty sunlight of the summer morning. From a long line of tall chimneys of varying heights a pretty smoke rolled out lazily ; between the chimneys, decorative towers and spires and blocks of massive buildings rose in masses of blue shadow touched with glints of golden light ; over all hovered a slender, white spire, an ephemeral expression of spiritual significance, a ghostly but lovely finger, white against the dark heat haze.

What was this enormous and strange city that looked so beautiful as it seemed to float on the glowing mist of a June morning ? Something delightfully dissipated and romantic from the Arabian Nights seemed only appropriate, and yet it was Preston. It might have been an Utopian centre of the Arts and Philosophy, but it was Preston—Preston, packed with a concentrated fury of manufacture, business, and

94

marketing, fighting for its life in the crude, savage struggle of seeing who can be richest.

We hoped that this was the last we should see of the Land of Chimneys. Wherever we had walked they had bristled in the scene. In themselves they are only slightly monstrous ; the smoke they deliver is definitely a poison, but the mills they spring out of are a perversion of all that is worth living for in this earthly life. I had never realised the exact meaning of having " been through the mill." I know now. Lancashire has been through the mill. Even its trees have never grown up, and the very grass suffers from under-nourishment. We had passed garden after garden and about the only flower to be seen was that very hardy perennial, the lupin ; to a great extent there had been no gardens, and not even lupins. And never had I seen so many short people, with pale, thin faces, with prematurely aged faces, lined and hard-bitten with overwork and extremely simple living. To see much more of it would start one thinking about life seriously, and that way lies madness. The mess, of course, is all being cleared up nowadays.

" Never have I known the Lancashire air so clear," remarked a chance acquaintance to us. " It's because so many mills are closed down, you know."

But besides that tragic assistance to the clearance there must have been some heroic work on the part of some peculiarly tough specimens of the genus social reformer. Bit by bit order and brightness are creeping into the ghastly accumulations of those wild and wicked Victorians. Our lane, as it neared Walton, gave up its attempt at pretending to be country ; new houses were being built, and not the old back to back cottages rising perpendicularly from narrow pavements, but semi-attached little houses with gardens, and children playing among the flowers, and one of them, a boy of eighteen months, stared at us and said, with extreme perspicacity for such an age, " What a foony cart ! "

And there were other, and older people, who also thought it was a funny cart. I had gone off to find a post office, leaving Winifred with the barrow, which she had pushed up by the side of a house, and, standing apart, she had suddenly heard our property being discussed by the inmates, in terms which she reports as follows :—

" Naw, muther, what d'ye think yon is ? "

" Nay, lad, ah 'aven't an earthly."

" Well, ah'm fair puzzled misel'."

" Summat ter do with an airyplane, laikely."

" Nay, ah 'ardly think so. But what are they pushing t'thing for ? "

" Must ha' summat ter do wi' theirsel's. Some folks seem to 'ave plenty o' time."

" And yer right theer, an' all. But ah'd be none too keen, misel', to be pushing that thing on t'road. It takes two on 'em to keep it fra' running down t'ills. Our Doreen seen 'em with it this morning. She thought it wa' some sort of a barril organ and wanted to axe 'em if they'd a munkey."

" Eh, it's a long time sin ah saw one of them munkeys. Right clever they are an' all. T'last ah saw wa' years ago at Blackpool. Theer wa' one as used to come up t'wall to t'winders and beg for coppers. Had a red coat on and a green cap, an' all."

" Aye, it's funny where all t'things get to. Don't see them okey-pokey men abaht, neether."

" Naw, these 'ere stop me and buy ones done for them, ah reckon."

" Aye, t'roads are full o' traffic these days. Too much on 'em in my opinion."

" Aye, that's it. Like old Belisha to come and sleep 'ere. These 'ere night lorries are something awful. Ah've 'ad one bit o' plaister on my 'ead in t'neet a'ready."

" Aye. Reminds yer o' t'war, don't it ? "

" Aye, summat always reminds yer o' summat else."

It was then, with the utterance of this sad but very true axiom, that the lady had actually remembered that she had baking to attend to, and went off ejaculating as to the condition of her bread.

As we progressed the summer morning changed its mind, and a blue-black gloom came down heavily on the world. Clouds of flies attacked us, and we had to wave a green bough round our heads continually. There are so few pedestrians and horses on the roads that the flies have to seize their opportunities. We must have been the first slow-moving traffic for a month, and some genius in Flytown must have been posting the walls with exhortations to *Eat More Humans*. They came down on us like a plague, buzzing and biting furiously, and to this accompaniment we ascended the hill beyond Walton in a sticky, thundery heat. We were beyond the houses at last. We looked down on the winding

Ribble and walked a quiet road of farmlands, a peaceful country road, with a wide grass verge to the sides. But we were not very peaceful. The blue-black gloom was ominous, and before the most frightful storm of the century broke I went across the fields to a farm in search of a pitch.

When I returned Winifred was in the hands of the police. There had been a local robbery, but whether we were suspected is not quite clear ; at all events an amiable discussion was in progress as to the behaviour of young excursionists to the country. We had noticed repeatedly that anything smashable set up on the roads was duly smashed. Anything in the way of a traffic sign had been showered with stones, and those little glass reflectors marking particular signs were invariably a complete ruin. " It's the lads from the towns," said the constable. " They want to get back to nature, but they don't know how to do it. It's pathetic ! "

The farmers, as usual, were very willing that we should camp on their ground and in the middle of their busy life. The farmer's wife was baking bread, preparing a meal, and superintending some workmen, but she took us in her stride, supplied milk and eggs, and after three minutes' acquaintance invited us to use the bathroom—or anything. We put up the tent very quickly and got inside. It was none too soon, for the rain came, and thunder and lightning, and a fitful breeze that every now and again through the night seized the tent and shook it as a dog shakes a rat.

I suppose we moved on with a simple belief in the future, that eventually the weather would become more settled and that there would be an opportunity for our affairs. At all events we were travelling forward to a more desirable country, and we had our pleasant moments, but travelling on that Saturday morning was not among them. We were meeting the week-end traffic coming over the Pennines from the Yorkshire towns to Blackpool, and a continual stream of coaches and private cars came swinging round the corners. The coaches came in duplicate and triplicate, varied with frequent lorries, broad of beam and piled terrifyingly high with swaying loads. In between were numbers of private cars that continually attempted to pass the lorries or the coaches. They swerved out from behind a vehicle, saw us in what remained of the road, and considerately retired again, or simply dashed ahead, clearing us and the lorry by an inch or two. This meant that we were forced to draw into the bank and, at times, to get the near wheel cocked up at a dangerous angle. Not for one minute could we relax to think about the charming birds or the dear little flowers ; our road sense was fully occupied. Of course, we ought to have been forcibly detained from pushing a barrow along that particular road on a Saturday morning. It was as perilous for the cars and coaches as it was for us ; any false move on our part might have produced a major catastrophe. It was a question of a fraction of an inch repeatedly. While Winifred propelled the barrow I concentrated upon preventing it from tipping into the road when we were forced to run one wheel on the bank. We studied the map anxiously for a side road, but there was not one before Mellor Brook, and all the way there we registered vows that this was the last time we would push a barrow on " ye olde roads of Englande." Mellor Brook is a junction of five roads, and after rounding a blind corner with extreme trepidation we came to the side turning. We shot into it, and were about to relax at last, when a following car trumpeted to us to get out of the way. We did. I can argue about the traffic problem in writing, but not on the road ; there is only one thing to do then—get out of the way.

I believe there are some instructions issued for the direction of pedestrians on the roads, but I cannot remember that they are at all sensible or adequate. A pedestrian's first requisite nowadays is that he should be a good jumper—a thorough steeplechaser. Let him have a capacity for leaping into stagnant ditches, or springing over high hedges, and he is tolerably safe. If he can dive, at a moment's notice, into a bramble bush or a bed of nettles, and come up smiling, he can account himself a good road pedestrian ; and he will be well consoled for any scratches or stings if one motorist in a dozen acknowledges his action with a graceful lift of the hand. If he can swarm a lamp-post or a handy tree swiftly, like Tarzan of the Apes, or cling to the face of a stone wall like a flattened limpet, he will not only save his skin, but, at times, will draw a rare smile from the passing driver. Most motorists, it is naturally granted, would like to be polite, but, of course, they are far too anxious to do anything but stare ahead and wonder when the bash is coming.

After this dismal experience we got into a meadow as

soon as we could, and roamed about the green pasture
in an ecstasy of freedom. It was quiet there, and we
looked out over the Ribble to Longridge Fell, deep in
the rural sanctity, far removed, thank goodness, from
Life. It is true we examined Mellor Brook again with
a performance in view, but the only possible pitch was
a yard, marked very plainly in splendid printing :
PRIVATE ENTRY. DON'T OBSTRUCK.

We looked again, just to make certain, and passed on
" inckstincktively." But the village shop was rich in
home-made cakes and pies, and in bottles of TIZER,
THE APPETISER, an innocuous liquor of sweet
fizz which calls to you from all the advertisement
hoardings along the Lancashire roads. With a load of
fizz and pies we retired to the meadow for the week-end,
wondering if the next week would at last bring the
summer weather.

Our farmer, the artful fellow, was busy all the
Saturday evening cutting grass, hoping that while he
rested on the Sunday the grass would make itself into
hay ready for him to carry on the Monday. He was
not an hereditary farmer. He had been a builder, but
having grown tired of living and working all over the
place, he had decided to turn farmer so that he could
live in one place. And he liked being a farmer. The
change had been hard work, but : " As I often say to
the missis, look at the milk we drink. Instead of a quart
a day we now have four or five and think nothing of it.
And the family eats dozens of eggs, and we don't count
them, but if I was on wages we'd have to look at every
one. And there's bacon and chickens—all we want."

H   101

He was a real backward fellow, like us, who had no admiration for modern improvements, but he sometimes walked up to the end of the road just to watch the traffic passing, and to wonder where it was all coming from and how so many people could afford to possess cars.

"Of course, there are not the children there used to be, and that makes a difference," he said. "Our school-teacher is getting nervous and thinks she'll be looking for a job in a few years. When I was a boy at Balderstone school there used to be about a hundred children. My boy goes now to the same school and there's only about thirty. And when I look round the district and count up, there's going to be fewer still later on."

Perhaps his prognostications were wrong. At all events Monday morning was so wet that his little plan of collecting the self-made hay was completely defeated. He spent his day in a shed sharpening the cutters of his machine, and we, unable to move our camp, took a bus into Blackburn with the desperate intention of hiring a caravan. A tent is quite a possible house in dry, fine weather, when you can spread out and be more out of the tent than in it. But when it rains continually and you are restricted to its narrow confines of a couple of yards, it ceases to be either amusing or practicable for more than a day. You spend your time reclining; you cook on all fours; you dress and undress in a stoop, and get through your toilet in a squat. You can never stand up, or walk, or lean against anything, or even do anything so ordinary as to sit on a chair. And eventually you retire into a sleeping-bag, dream the hours away in a snug coma, and find yourself lunching at half-past four and taking afternoon tea at eight in the evening. A lethargy creeps into your limbs from inactivity ; your morals go to pieces, and you—well—not so much refuse as forget to wash up, and eat out of the hand. And have not the slightest inclination to notice where the banana skins go to. You do not suffer from discomfort so much as from too much comfort. You are warm, the senses become dimmed, and you are easily pleased. At the last moment of utter boredom you find a sheet of old newspaper round the spring onions, and after reading last week's Stock Exchange prices, which mean nothing to you, and a company report or two, and the financial news from Wall Street, which is all gibberish as far as you are concerned, having no finance to worry about, you are sufficiently refreshed to roll over on the other side and chase a black beetle out of the hamper.

So, we went into Blackburn with the intention of finding a caravan in which, we imagined, we could live a more moral life, or travel on whether it rained or not. It might even prove a necessity, and become a refuge, a Noah's Ark to save us from the phenomenal rainfall. After a few unsuccessful inquiries we were so wet that we turned into a café, where, seated on chairs and with our feet on a dry carpet, we thought of the tent and listened with profound joy to the wet waters rushing down on Blackburn. The roofs streamed with water ; the streets ran rivers. It was the deluge, but we had our feet on the dry carpet, and for all we cared the tent might have been flattened down to the level of the earth beneath this extraordinary weight of water.

There was no orchestra, but the waitresses kept us well entertained with a loud conversation in between carrying the dishes.

" 'Ave you seen Elsie Tiddleboddle lately ? "

" 'Er ? No, I ain't seen 'er."

" What's become of 'er boy ? "

" 'Im ? Oh, I seen 'im. 'E goes aht wi' Annie Widdlewaddle now, you know."

" I thought she went out wi' Ernie Fiddlefaddle ! "

" Oh, that was last month. I saw Lucy Mackers last night at the pictures."

" 'Er ? What's she doing nowadays ? "

" I dunno."

There was more rain than Blackburn, and our view of it was very restricted. And there were more inquiries than caravans, and in the end we decided to return to Mellor Brook and advance ourselves beyond a caravan to a house until the waters subsided. But as we came out of Blackburn to the country the earth and the air brightened. A silvery sparkle showed through the rain and the grass was very green. On the other hand, lodgings looked exceedingly dismal, of the linoleum and aspidistra kind, and we passed on to the tent to find it still standing and perfectly dry, and clean and bright. At nine o'clock a weird burst of sunlight, a mixture of midday and midnight, a thing of stormy gloom and ghostly brightness, frightened us out of our lives, it was so unearthly. But we slept in the tent and waited on the morrow with open minds.

XI

RIBCHESTER GETS A BOB

WE did not move until the second day. Even then the morning was gloomy, thundery, and suffused with hot moisture, and we were aware that Lancashire can have a west country lethargy. We had no gas oven to put our heads into, and the Meta fuel had run low. There was only the miserable little primus stove that would have needed more persistence than we possessed to finish things off effectively, and our knives were of the sixpenny store variety. There was nothing for it but to move on, and we found the road very uncomfortable with swift traffic, until we mounted the footpath that was kerbed and cindered and, weirdly enough, entirely free from pedestrians. We were safe, if illegal, on the footpath, and I am sure the road was safer for our absence. It would have been entirely a pleasure to have been fined for so trespassing to everybody's advantage.

We were undecided as to whether we were going to Whalley and Pendle Hill or Ribchester, until we shopped from a couple at a corner, who were enthusiastic about the view from their shop, hidden in gloom at the moment, and thought that Ribchester was as fine as anything the Lakes could show. That decided us. The awful weather had no intention of allowing us to wander carelessly, and if we were to penetrate the northern lands of the county it was obvious that we must steer persistently in that direction without erratic divergences. We had seen Pendle Hill from Balderstone, a bold cone rising prominently, and regretted having to leave it on our right. But we were penetrating the real country now, and any road east, west, or north would have carried us to the hilly and rural loveliness of northern England.

The Ribchester road was quiet, and for the first time of the journey we really relaxed and enjoyed the expansive freedom of being " in the country." Two horse-drawn vehicles jogged past us, and these were followed by a pedestrian carrying a verdant armful of plants for the garden, I'm sure. The grass was greener and thicker, and the trees were more packed with leaves. More coloured flowers were in the green hedgerow, and altogether there was an exhilarating sense of the power to live and grow, to wax fat and colourful, to feel gloriously idle and pleasant, and to open the mind to wandering thoughts and influences. At the top of the hill down into Ribchester we stood entranced, for here the world spread itself before us, a green valley with wide pastures and handsome masses of trees, and the invisible tentacles of our beings could reach out to the sky and over this great scene, drawing the mysterious sustenance that had been denied us among the curses of civilisation, that amusing name given to overcrowding and all the consequently invented intricacies that attempt to make it possible, but only succeed in making it worse.

Descending the hill, we came on Mr. Danson diligently hoeing the weeds out of the cinder footpath, and we asked his advice about roads, thinking that his work would have given him a good experience, and he encouraged our choice of route. I forget how we advanced to higher things, but Danson had suddenly ceased from hoeing, and was leaning handsomely on his implement, as Wolsey might have leaned on anything that was handy on the stage, and declaiming :

" Mark but my fall, and that that ruined me.
   Cromwell, I charge thee, fling away ambition."

Recollecting himself, he smiled, continued hoeing, and said :

" This is the best job I ever had—gives me time to think. When you're among a crowd you haven't time to enjoy yourself."

He hoed vigorously while he asked us to look at the feverish careers of public men, and the misery of being successful, and the agony of always trying to be more successful.

" And what is it all for ? Far better do nowt than struggle to get money that you never have the time or the sense to enjoy."

He leaned on his hoe again and broke out into a rhapsody.

" I remember, once, being on the Northumberland moors. I was lying in the heather, and there was the sea, and the sky, and all the lovely colour, you know. I was just lying in the sun, doing nowt, and it was quiet !—you could hear nowt but now and then just one peewit, perhaps. Ee ! it wur grand. I thowt it wur heaven, and just wished it could go on for ever."

As he continued to hoe he told us how he liked poetry, and having a good memory had learned a great deal by heart, which he could say over to himself as he worked. Gray's *Elegy* was perhaps his favourite poem. He found something in it that spoke to every mood, and found himself saying it over many times in the day. He did not think such a poem could be written nowadays : " There was not the time to understand nature or to be attuned to it." And two other poems stood out in his mind, *The Task*, and that sensitive piece, *On the Receipt of my Mother's Picture out of Norfolk*.

We explained our errant ways to him and, naturally, he approved of them. He liked a free life, and often envied the tramp because he could take his own time about things.

" There's a bit of a jingle I picked up somewhere. I don't hardly know as how I remember it, like, but it wur something like this :

> " ' Of all the trades in England
> Abegging is the best,
> For when you are aweary,
> You can lay you down and rest.
>
> I begged for my old master,
> And got him store of pelf.
> But now, O God be thankit,
> I'm begging for myself.' "

Danson, the hoer, working so quietly on that hill-top above the wide green valley, almost restored our faith in the human animal, that he might, if he only gave his mind to it, be quite a decent, sensitive, and well-behaved affair. At all events he had given us a song, and we went on towards Ribchester, past the handsome old New Hall, grey stone and strong, by the De Tabley Arms, aristocratic and distinguished, and over the stone bridge across the Ribble, jingling, as the wheels went round :

> Of all the trades in England,
> Pup' showing is the best,
> For you never are aweary,
> And never stop to rest.
>
> We've wandered on, and on, and on,
> To here from Manchester,
> To be, before the sun goes down,
> In good old Ribchester.

Coming into the little town, we moved from wonder to wonder, and by degrees stole back into ancient days as we penetrated that winding street of seventeenth- and eighteenth-century houses, and the minute square with the old White Bull Inn, its overhanging upper story supported by four handsome stone pillars, and a large effigy of the White Bull himself proudly surveying the little square. The footways were all cobbles, light grey pebbles from the river bed with a semicircle of white before the doors, and often, between the white and the grey, an intervening inlay of pink pebbles.

Then we came out to the River Ribble—ribbling quietly by, as one might say—and from its curving bank you can sit and look up the green wooded valley enclosed with the gentle hills. It is difficult to believe that the Romans built a granary and a fort here for strategic reasons ; obviously it was only an excuse for the delight of living in that valley. But the Romans had been there, as its name and the present museum and all the remains it houses will testify.

The compact village with its central triangular square was the ideal pitch that we had been looking for, and we set out to find a camp, determined to return in the evening with the theatre. As we went through the street to the fields the employees were coming in from the two silk factories, which, being Lancashire, must, of course, be there with tall chimneys all complete. But what a music we walked through ! It was the March of the Revolution ! It was the music of Great Events ! It was the Oncoming of the Proletariat ! It was the clippety-clop of hundreds of iron-shod wooden clogs on the cobbles of Ribchester, and the great event was the dinner hour. In that mighty symphony we were excited to think of the good audience that would gather round the puppets in the evening, and we pushed on, to establish the tent in a high meadow, a pleasant field above the valley and the hills.

After some tea I went down to the village with the show. It was a glorious evening and I sailed down the hill full of pleasant anticipations. As a preliminary the landlord of the White Bull took a shilling off me as rent for the pitch, the village square, or rather triangle, being his car-park, and I began setting up the theatre. Some youths were interested and a good crowd of children gathered round.

" If you start oop, like, they'll coom round," said the optimistic landlord with my shilling in his pocket, and I started " oop like." I could see the street dimly through the curtains, and well enough to notice that most of the doors along the street held a spectator, and that a few were peeping over window curtains—very cautious observers, these. A few adults stood at awkward places, too proud to approach something that attracted them, but which was, presumably, for children. The performance pursued its normal course, and the audience, which was amused and interested, seemed to grow larger. There was a coming and going of passers-by, but, as far as I could perceive through the curtains, there was always a fair crowd, the children in front, the adults at odd places, and the spectators at the doors. I brought the performance, a good long one, to a conclusion, and went out with the hat to make a collection.

And now, where was this audience that I flattered myself was listening with attention to my efforts ? Every door in the street was closed, and the peepers over window curtains had ducked out of sight pretty quickly. I could see the elbow of a man, round the corner of a house, who, I was convinced, had watched the performance from the beginning. But before the theatre were only the children, a youth or two, and two or three giggling maidens, a group that did not encourage the idea of a collection, and I decided not to proffer the hat. I began to pack instead, and I went on packing ; but all that happened was that the children began to take liberties with the theatre, banging the curtains, pushing each other into them, and pitching stones into the proscenium. On being reproved they moved off sulkily. The maidens went over to the sweet shop and made purchases, but not a single acid drop was offered to the showman who had amused them.

Gradually the square emptied until I was left with four very small children, who could not speak, try as I might to win their confidence. Finally they departed and I was alone in the square, surrounded by the closed doors, the vacant windows, and the empty street. No one spoke to me. There was no ribaldry, thanks, or curiosity. Not a word. I was particularly disappointed in the landlord of the inn, who, I thought, might have offered me a drink. I finished the packing in the empty square, under the sign of the White Bull, the regardless, simpering effigy, that was more like a cow than a bull. It was not until I was completely packed and about to leave that a man appeared in the square, approached, and asked amiably enough where I was making for, and what was I doing. But I very much suspect that he was a policeman—without his war-paint.

So Ribchester had scored off me quite handsomely. The landlord had got his shilling, the children a show and I walked out so much the worse. It was interesting. I have given hundreds of such impromptu performances but never before, in any part of England, had I been allowed to go off without a collection, or without some member of the audience wanting to talk to me. Gypsies in the New Forest had insisted upon collecting among themselves after a show ; a village in Yorkshire in which I did not collect was highly indignant, and did the job for me. Possibly the inhabitants of Ribchester were bashful, and I expect my southern accent was thought affected, and " a bit soft." And, of course, times had been bad in Lancashire—yes—but, it is possible to speak to an inoffensive stranger without parting with anything. Had I started a collection I might have gone out of Ribchester simply rolling with wealth ; as it was, I went out with the feeling that if the inhabitants of Ribchester are so very cautious they will not only save themselves from being cheated, but from being blessed as well.

Can it be that modern Ribcastrians have inherited the business capacity of their Roman ancestors, who, according to an account, quoted from Tacitus by F. A. Bruton, had some sharp practices with regard to granaries, such as the one which had been at Ribchester.

" If the Britons," he tells us, " had no corn as tribute, they were compelled to stand outside the Roman granary and bid against one another for the corn stored there, till the price had reached an absurd figure, and then to pay the corn so purchased as tribute, the corn never having left the granary at all."

It was a very different jingle that carried me away from the village, to the one that carried us into it :

> Of all the towns in England
> That least deserves our thanks,
> Is dear old stingy Ribchester
> Down on the Ribble banks.

XII

SIDELIGHTS ON RIBCHESTER

THE high camp above Ribchester was delightful. It was one of those camps that we regretted leaving, the sort of meadow for whose short clean blades of grass and little daisies we came to have an affection. It was so clean and sweet-smelling, and you could see so far across the country, across the Ribble to Mellor, where we had camped the night before, and down the valley to Stonyhurst College, whose grey buildings stood out in the clear day among the green fields and woods. We remarked to the farmer that he had a lovely pitch. " So they tell me," he said. " But I was born over there, and now I live here, and I suppose we don't notice it." He indicated two houses about four fields apart. But our hosts were properly interested in the camp. While I had been in the village Winifred had been making a drawing, and every one had come to see it, and had then sent every one else. And the farmer, who had collected his sheep out of the meadow to treat them for " ticks," was suddenly fearful lest he had ruined the drawing by taking away the foreground. We were regretful to leave it, but we went, and wandered along in thundery heat towards Longridge, until we met a travelling greengrocer and bought a refreshing basket of strawberries. He was an honest

fellow, and refused to sell us his carrots and cauli-
flowers, because, he said : " they are not worth the
money."

" I can tell you don't come from these parts," he
said, " by your speech. It isn't Lancashire talk ; not
that Lancashire people talk Lancashire nowadays. I
don't know what it is they do speak. A sort of half and
half, and God meant nothing to be half and half."

I thought he looked rather expectant when he asked
how we had got on in Ribchester ; he was certainly
amused when he did hear the story. " Ah ! You
could go a hundred miles and not meet another place
like Ribchester. Everybody knows everybody else's
business, like all these small towns, and I always say if
anyone hurts their foot in Ribchester the whole town
limps."

A stiff hill brought us into Longridge and, Winifred
not feeling well, we turned into the White Bull Inn,
where a clever landlady improvised a vegetarian lunch
on the spur of the moment, and dispensed unalcoholic
liquor with a perfect sang-froid, an heroic deed which
is second only to a teetotaler asking you which kind of
expensive wine you prefer. When sufficiently recovered
we went into the bar to pay and encountered two
gentlemen enjoying a midday pint. One of them smiled
affectionately and I suddenly recognised inside the
neat lounge suit a man, in messy overalls, I had spoken
with the evening before, and the other, I soon learned,
had seen the fun in Ribchester. He had been having
his shave in the barber's, and along with other customers
had watched the show over the curtain. He was one

of the peepers who had ducked when I came out with the hat ! As I turned to pay he began saying to his companion, " and, you know, it was a good show, a grand show—" but noticing that Winifred was listening he cut short his eulogium, and, turning to her, said :

" You know, we always say it costs eighteenpence to get a shilling out of Ribchester. You ought to have advertised the performance and then all the town would have come. They would have flocked to it and —you might have made a shilling ! Not long ago one of the parliamentary candidates came to Ribchester to speak. He came unannounced with a whacking great car and a loud speaker—and he got an audience of four. You did better than that. You know, I had an old friend who used to say that if he had a son to educate he would send him to Manchester Grammar School, to Stonyhurst, to Oxford or Cambridge, and then send him to finish his education with a year in Ribchester ! "

It was a pity that we had not heard all this before attempting a show in Ribchester, but I know if there is ever another performance in that melancholy street the first act will be a collection. I have noticed since that it seems to be the fashion in Lancashire, and, incidentally, during these weeks of travel we had seen not one single itinerant street musician in any village or town. I suppose, like the music-hall comedians, they all come *out* of Lancashire, but never in.

It was pleasant walking through Longridge, which we found to be a busy little place. The baker supplied us with those fresh-made biscuits, and pies, and a cake, and the grocer, who was sitting on his steps playing with a kitten, found useful things in his stock for us, and when he heard that we were about to walk through the Trough of Bowland, he uttered the word "beautiful" in every possible variety of tone. Bowland was beautiful, in a dulcet tenor; it was beautiful, in an awestruck bass ; it was beautiful, in a smiling baritone ; it was beautiful anyhow, and we were to be sure not to miss the chapel there, which had been built to commemorate a racehorse, he said. Having restored its master's fortunes by winning the Derby, and everything else, thanks had been returned in the shape of the chapel. " There used to be a plaque of the horse over the altar," said our informant, " but it has been removed."

Then there were the lettuces which we bought for twopence apiece. They would have been the mysterious amount of fivepence, I feel sure, anywhere in the south, but " that's all they'll pay round here," said the shopwoman. " And then they've a fixed idea that a lettuce only ought to be a penny."

This shopping in Longridge was important because we were going on to pass a long week-end, at least, in the wilds, and were not sure when we would encounter another shop. We were making for Bowland Forest, which you will see on the contour map as a vast, very brown district, meaning that it is high. There is only one road across it, the famous Trough of Bowland, or the " Truff of Bolland," as we were learning to call it, and, for the rest, it is all moorland, with sparsely inhabited valleys, and villages far apart.

In the meantime we walked out of Longridge in a delightful afternoon, out of the mixed-up Longridge with its rank of old severe cottages on the summit of the hill and its blossoming modernity nearer the main road, into the real and pleasant country under Long-ridge Fell, where there were the groups of quiet cattle under the trees and distant sheep on the fellside. Haymakers were in the sunny fields surrounding the neat grey farms, and about the bright fields rose the graceful ash tree, and the dark and shapely sycamore, as precisely designed and drawn as those decorative trees in a Persian manuscript. It was easy walking, and we drifted on delightfully between the hedgerows, turning over the high ground at the end of the Fell, and what could be more appropriate than to walk into a large farmyard, full of the singing of boys as they milked the cows in the shippons, to ask for a camp. The farm was one of the old Halls of the countryside, a large house with a handsome front, and two very tall cut trees on either side of the entrance. A handsome house, not of this age, and only preserved by its own power and dignity that Time could make shabby and neglected, but could not efface.

We were put into a paddock that poised us charmingly over the vale of Chipping, and as we went about our business the evening closed in over the old village under the high fells, and the rich light flooded the valley with limpid gold. Wherever you looked in that wide scene were pictures and compositions: grey farms and dark, designed trees ; shapely meadows between the hedges and walls, and more trees ; the various fells

118

growing mysterious, and wilder in the sinking light.
And it all grew quiet and still, so that you heard a
distant dog bark from the opposite side of the vale, or
a small human voice float up from a tiny farm.

In the paddock was an astonishing family of chickens,
cocks, geese, ducks, and a score of comic, ceaselessly
busy, yellow ducklings. With incredible energy they all
searched for minute specks of food, appearing in the
vicinity of the tent at regular intervals of about half an
hour ; a restless, searching army pecking morsels of
nothing the whole time. The geese walked by us, heads
in air, screaming fearful defiance ; the chickens paused
a moment, blinked, and then went on pecking ; the
cocks hovered about, looking for a chance to fight, but
the twenty ducklings rediscovered the tent each time
with a frightful clamour, and nibbled the guy-lines, the
blocks, the pegs, the hanging tapes, anything that was
biteable in the hopes of finding something good to eat.

It was during one of the quiet periods that we noticed
in the mouth of the tent the extraordinary phenomenon
of a moth emerging from its chrysalis. The new, raw
creature left its case, climbed a blade of grass and
trembled delicately while its creased wings unfolded,
and its large eyes looked out greedily to Life. As the
evening was turning chilly and the grass damp, we were
concerned for the comfort of this intricate and fragile
miracle clinging to its bit of grass, and attempted to
bring it into the shelter of the tent. But it was so
flustered by our suggestion that we abandoned the
effort and left it to develop on its own responsibility.
It trembled ; its wings uncreased, and spread them-

selves until you could see every minute piece of structure and variation of colour, and even all the hundreds of absurdly tiny hairs. We discussed some sort of protection for it during the night ; could we feed it ? What would it like to drink ? Would it care for a little music ? What could we do for this morsel of creation that seemed to have fallen into our charge. We did nothing. The matter was taken out of our hands entirely, for a small yellow duckling suddenly shot his gobbling bill round the corner of the tent, and the new moth, all that wonderful and intricate miracle, after less than an hour of earthly joys, was miraculously incorporated in the duck. Art is long, but Life, in the shape of a duckling, can be very swift and devastating. The incident unsettled us, because, however careful and good a creature, even a human creature, may be, there is always the possibility of a nasty duck round the next corner.

We went on. It was a grey morning, the dewy haze before the heat, and we walked the real country at last, with occasional rabbits lolloping from hedge to hedge, and the curlew crying over the fields. The road wound between the hedges from farm to farm, the high hill of Longridge Fell mistily above us, and the lower fields pretty with mixed families of cattle and chickens, fading away into the misty valley. You could feel the quietness of it, and every cock-crow and curlew cry, every sheep and cow noise were all subdued harmoniously into the serenity of the wide-spreading fields and hills. There was a lull in the morning. The milking was done, and the beasts fed. The farmers were standing about doing odd jobs ; one was sharpening his grass cutter ; another was examining a sick sheep ; three together were discussing a horse that stood patiently, one of the friendly group. We had the road to ourselves, a road pretty with the wild flowers and strawberries among the decorative grasses, and with honeysuckle and wild roses over our heads.

We did meet two Irish labourers that walked in and out of our world, quite casually, with an enormous story. Thirty miles they had tramped the day before, and had spent the night under a hedge. No one would employ them. They were not known in the district, and before engaging the farmers wanted to know every incident of their careers. It is difficult to get to the bottom of this employment business. We were always hearing of farmers who could not get labour, and of labourers who could not get farmers, and probably neither wanted either. There was a lot of talk and fencing, and evidently a great waste of time. In the meantime the labourers took some cigarettes off us.

The climax of this delightful road—a poem, a diamond, a rose compared with those ghastly by-pass affairs of which all really important people are so proud nowadays—the climax of it was Doeford Bridge, where we lingered over the wide, rocky bed of the River Hodder. The wide, shallow waters rippled under the overhanging trees, setting up that persistent river music, the gentle, limpid murmur of water running over stones. The wagtails posed on stones, flicking their tails incessantly, while the dippers went up and down, and under the bridge, and at intervals a trout leapt for his fly. The rest of the world was so still, so quiet, the patient trees, the standing hills, the dewy fields, all waiting on the running river, the ever-flowing water that had been singing the same song since forded by the Romans there. We wandered about the bridge, leaning over one side and the other, now in Lancashire and now in Yorkshire, for the county boundary runs across the middle of the bridge, a line where the smooth road of Lancashire ended and the rough new road of Yorkshire began.

So we walked over the bridge into Yorkshire, an odd projecting piece of the county, and proceeded through a quiet open country surrounded by misty hills. Before us it was all a minor Switzerland, with numbers of sharp-pointed hills rising above sloping meadows and clumps of pine trees, while behind were the higher hills, appearing the larger and more mysterious on account of the enveloping mists. It was a warm, misty day, a little unreal, and the vague hills before us suggested a wild world's end of primeval rocks and virgin forest. It was delightful. We thought of bears and bandits, but retained sufficient mental balance to know that they were imaginary. In a wood we came back to the river, swirling round a bend under a steep hanger of trees, and we followed by its side to Whitewell, to the large respectable hotel that suggested a comfortable Victorian foundation, and took its place restfully in the masses of trees at that picturesque corner among the sharp little hills. Whitewell is a rich and sheltered refuge in that country, a comfortable hostel where, one imagines, luxurious anglers may spend ten pounds a week, and enjoy entrancing days in the rippling river under the trees, catching six penn'orth of fish.

We wandered about looking for a good camp. The next stage of our journey was to climb the Trough of Bowland, and we had been warned that the week-end traffic would make the road impossible for us. The Trough of Bowland excited us. Frequently eyebrows had shot up at the idea of pulling the barrow over there, and every one impressed upon us its attractiveness and the flood of traffic that would be making its way there on the Sunday. So we turned off the main road, and hid ourselves in the recesses of a farm on the quieter road to Chipping. Nothing could have been quieter than that remote farm, farmed by an elderly couple who had spent their days in the vale and recognised it as the most important centre of the universe. They strayed to Clitheroe on market days, but returned to their native fields with relief. Nowadays they used a car and made the journey in a few hours, but in their younger days it had meant getting up at four o'clock. They grumbled, but, at least when the mornings were fine, it must have been a precious experience to drive through the ten miles or so of green dales to the market. Life had an heroic quality in those days of the horse and the legs. Think of the youth of that district, who, after making the market journey to Clitheroe with horse and cart and back to the farm, had then spent the evening in walking back to Clitheroe to court a girl. And in the end he had not married the girl. But on second thoughts I suppose a young fellow would do as much nowadays, would willingly mount the motor cycle and ride a hundred miles in the evening to have ten minutes with a girl in a tobacconist's kiosk.

The Sunday was a far-away day. The farmers had gone off to a christening, and we sat under the plum trees in the orchard of the deserted farm, with the hills towards Slaidburn before us and a steep hanger above. The day was one of those miraculous water-colours of Turner done mysteriously in about three insignificant, blobby washes of delicate colour ; but it was all there, the hills and the dales, faint in the sunny mist, infinitely lovely with an entrancing subtlety and delicacy. We could hear the faint and continual throb of the traffic, and in the afternoon we wandered off to see it, and to take a preliminary survey of this " Truff " that we were to pull up the next day.

The entrance to the pass was through a five-bar gate across the road which went on romantically through the open bracken and pasture. The gate was opened very politely by an old fellow who was suitably rewarded. There was a swing gate to the side for pedestrians, and at a pinch we could have opened the five-bar gate, but he insisted, and as strangers we naturally deferred and produced the tip. Of course it would never do to leave the gate open and allow all the sheep to escape from the fells. What we could see of the road did not look impossible, and, ignoring the notices not to do so, we climbed the hill-side a bit and perched ourselves among the bracken, the bedstraw and thyme, watching the procession of vehicles below us, and very glad to see the popularity of the Trough working itself off on the Sunday.

We ambled about the hill-sides and down by the river until we encountered a cottage that invited us to tea. The door was opened by an old gentleman, who called out to the interior of the house in an exasperated voice, " 'Ere's two more of 'em ! " We were then faced by a severe and very large lady, who asked if we wanted a " full " tea, or just tea with, perhaps, some fruit. We decided for " just tea," and were conducted by the exasperated gentleman through the coal cellar, the cleanest and whitest you ever saw, to the front parlour.

And what a tea was set before us presently ! It was a model for all caterers, and its like should be compulsory throughout the land. First, with intense care and interest, a sufficiency of plates and tackle was laid out on a spotless white cloth. Then was set, in exactly the right position, a crisp lettuce fresh from the garden, with hard-boiled egg and dressing ; followed a large plate of home-made brown and white bread and butter ; then a plate of pleasantly assorted small cakes, currant pasty, jam pasty, courting cakes and apple pies, and a real sponge sandwich, jam, a bowl of fruit salad, and finally, all piping hot, a large brown pot of tea. You eat as much as you can, you are asked if you would like any more, and without any quizzing as to how much you have eaten you are charged the sensational sum of one shilling and threepence. And you are so pleased that you feel like doing it all over again.

This remarkable tea was enjoyed in the company of an equally remarkable and enjoyable couple, an elderly man and his wife. Outwardly they were completely unsensational ; a tidy, modest couple typical of a small

Lancashire town. That afternoon they had come from Clitheroe by bus to Whitewell, had walked across the river fields to Dunsop Bridge, and after the good tea would walk back to Clitheroe by a road over the fells rising to a thousand feet. And they walked off into the rich gold of the evening sun, the green gold hills about them, laying up a store of quiet refreshment to carry them through the next week's work. Every week-end they made such an expedition, and had quietly walked hundreds of miles together to every point of the compass. And long may they walk those paths among the dales under the hills of Lancashire and Yorkshire. They must be among the last of the pedestrians, and a statue to them would not be inappropriate.

XIII

DROWNED IN THE TROUGH

THERE was a grim note about our packing on the Monday morning when we prepared for this pass ahead, which had occasioned so often that thoughtful question, with an earnest glance at the barrow, " And are you going to pull that oop Truff ? " We saw that the load was balanced precisely, that all straps were secure, the wheels well greased, and ourselves in the proper sober state of mind. We were going up the Trough. We might have been setting out for Everest.

The morning was the usual non-committal, hesitating, misty indecision of grey vapour, slightly committed, if anything, to a depression moving in our direction, but we had little hope of performing anywhere and could concentrate on the walking, which rain might make uncomfortable but not impossible.

We cleared Dunsop Bridge and came to the carefully guarded gate of yesterday, which was now unguarded and open to the wide ; evidently without the least need of a guardian when there were not many pennies to be gained. And we walked that hedgeless road above the river, now up, now down, this switchback way carrying us slowly into the narrower confines of the hills. The hills were bare, and the world lonely, and except for the very pleasant surface of the road we might have been walking in any age. That pleased us ; to have nothing but the hill-sides clothed with bracken about us, and a rough river below was the correct scene, and our barrow with its tent and food seemed a more welcome companion. And how pleasant it was where we descended a steep hill, and the valley widened, and there was some level turf by the clear stream, and when, as we idled by the running waters, a baker's van drove into this primitive scene with pies and tarts and rolls and Eccles cakes, both the puffy ordinary kind and the flat, old-fashioned " sad " cakes.

The baker was a cheerful fellow and would have sold us enough stuff to last a month without the slightest ill-feeling, but he also amused us with his account of the keepers of the various gates across the road along which we had passed. It seems that these polite guardians can collect anything up to three pounds at a week-end. The rights are in the hands of the farmers, but the actual guardianship is done by casual fellows, mostly of the kind who collect at the week-end and spend the rest of the week in " blueing " the collection.

It was, in fact, so pleasant at this corner that we forgot the weather until large spots of rain began to fall on our Eccles cakes, and we noticed a heavy, moist-looking cloud curling over the brow of the fells. Our idle moments were over. We started walking again. The valley narrowed and we were shut in beneath the steep hills together with the road, the charming brook —and the rain, which had now settled down into a steady and stupid application of water where it was obvious water already existed in abundant quantities.

We noted the delightful pieces of turf by the brook where camping would have been a joy, but in this wild country where camping would have been natural, and might even have been necessary, were large notice-boards shouting at us, NO CAMPING, and warning us not to wander more than so many feet from the road.

It was obvious that we must keep walking. Those barren hill-sides and odd pieces of wild grass might have been under a glass case for all the use they were to us. I sometimes think that the only freedom left in this country is the freedom to talk about freedom ; in the meantime notices are stuck up everywhere confining one to the straight and narrow road. Anyhow, by this time we were so wet that the only possible plan was to keep walking until we dried or came to an inn. Everything was very wet. The road ran with a surface of water, the rocks dripped and streamed miniature waterfalls, and the brook began to swell visibly and gurgle audibly. So we splashed on between the polite notices of NO CAMPING, with uncomfortable chilly spots creeping into our clothing. Our shining hats were streaming water off in cascades over the brims, and the wind carried the drops into our ears and down our necks.

Ahead we could see the road mounting steadily before us in a series of sharp banks. This, we thought, must be the beginning of the awesome pass, and, conserving our energy carefully, we mounted in carefully planned stages and rests. We mounted in the rain, and we rested in the rain, and pulled on again through the cold, wet drops that descended in lines making a forest of streaming rain. It was stiff pulling, but we hauled steadily, carefully, keeping our strength in reserve for the final pull. What had they said ? There were two miles of this sort of thing ? That is to say another hour of the slow, heavy tugging process beneath the dripping rain. We must go on. NO CAMPING bawled the notices, NO CAMPING, and another trickle of rain went down one's back. We pulled up another rise and rested again. Before us a bank rose and turned a corner, and we wondered what awful chasms and gradients would be revealed. We mounted slowly, oh ! so carefully, rounded the corner, and the gradient lessened. In about two minutes we were amazed to find ourselves looking over a large country at our feet. It was absurd—we were at the summit. Our breath was unimpaired and our minds prepared for another hour of heroism. It was a shock, but we had climbed the Trough.

We began the descent, down the lovely tree-covered road, with the river running among the rocks under the trees. The rain splashed off the trees and had no mercy on us. Our boots were full of water. Our legs were wet. Hats, and the shoulders of our coats, and the pockets were all leaking, and still it rained and rained. There was no house—only the wet country and the streaming water. We came to a thick tree, a miraculous tree under which there was some shelter, and we were able to shake the water out of our things and comb the hair out of our eyes. But we had to go on. It was not without its attraction. A silvery brightness gleamed on the road and the grass, and the road by the brook

under the trees with its mosses and ferns among the
rocks was lovely.

Down we went. Down, down into a new world on
the northern side of the Trough, a wide country of
rolling hills, and the grand, rainy rampart of Bowland
Forest behind us. In an hour or so it grew more
civilised and we inquired about refreshments, or a bed
for the night. There was nothing to be had about there,
and we wandered on until the weight of the barrow
increased and a reluctance crept into our legs. Again
we inquired for bed or camp, but were informed that
neither was possible. Inns did not exist and camping
was prohibited. We were walking through a large
estate, and among those hundreds of acres a couple of
square yards could not be ours.

We were aggrieved. It was ridiculous. It was an
insult to two respectable, decent citizens to be denied a
couple of yards of dirt on which to camp for a few
hours. There we stood in the rain, dripping with wet,
the long road to Lancaster going on before us over a
bare moor a thousand feet above the sea. We were wet,
tired, and hungry ; there were many fields in which
we could have camped harmlessly, but it was not
allowed. NO CAMPING ! Had we been stray dogs
there might have been some pity for us. But we were
free human beings and could do as we liked. We were
free to walk back ten miles to Whitewell, or ten miles
forward to Lancaster. We were free to move on, anyhow, and to keep to the straight and narrow way between
the notices. We turned down a side road that we hoped
would lead us off this estate, and take us to some free,

simple farmers with some compassion and kindness behind their waistcoats. But this impersonal " estate " was interminable, and after more refusals we set out to walk until we came to an inn—or dropped.

It was a mile or so before the village with the whimsical name of Dolphinholme that a small sign caught our glance and directed us up a hill through a wood to *The Friends Meeting House and School, Wyresdale.* It looked attractive, and where Friends were we imagined intelligence, certainly kindness, and possibly freedom to camp. The little road was hilly, but we staggered along and found it leading through gates and into open fields, until, coming out to a sort of green at the top of the hill, we saw away to our right a farm, an obvious school, and one more house. Inquiries led us to the house, and we knocked at the door. It was a respectable door and the garden was very tidy. Our hats were bent and dripping—Winifred's had been climbing her head all the afternoon with shrinkage, and now perched instead of fitted. Our coats were sagging and our boots were clammy, sodden with water. By this time we were tired and shapeless with the effort of pushing. The villa door and the trim garden reduced us to sloppy, baggy, dishevelled tramps. You could hardly tell which was Winifred and which was Walter ; we were a couple of bundles of old, wet clothes.

As the door was opened by Miss Troup, the mistress of the school, I very skilfully manœuvred to a position behind Winifred, who thus had the honour of explaining our predicament. Within three seconds Miss Troup had said quietly, " Won't you come in ? " as if it were an entirely common occurrence for such tramps and entire strangers to ask for her hospitality. And at the end of five seconds we were saved! Miss Troup had recklessly offered us a room.

Dried, warmed, and fed, and having propitiated Miss Troup by the offer of a performance to her school, we began to discover our more normal selves. We sat round a fire with great talkings and, now that we were safe, boasted of how we had walked over the Trough in pouring rain. And we learned about this far-away Quaker school about which there was little to learn, except that the meeting-house must have originated many years ago, perhaps in the days of George Fox himself, who, of course, was familiar with all this country. The modern school had been grafted on to the old meeting-house and now served the district, about two dozen children wandering in from the farms around ; and in spite of their varying ages, sexes, and degrees of advancement, were all taught by the heroic and gracious Miss Troup.

The barrow and the tent amused themselves in the school shed, while we walked upstairs with candles, to sleep in beds high and dry above the sodden ground and well protected from the loose and sullen sky. It was a miraculous end to the trying day, and a triumphant escape from the inhospitable estate ; moreover, on these remote hill-tops, from where you could look over many miles of country to Morecambe Bay, we were happy to find at work an outlying post of the sensible spiritual life.

XIV

BYWAYS ROUND LANCASTER

BLACK and awful were the clouds that rolled over the hills the next morning and heavy the rain that beat against the window panes instead of our tent roof. We avoided thinking of the future and of how we were going to travel on ; for the moment there was breakfast at a table, and after that we offered to start the day's schooling with a performance of the puppets in the schoolroom.

The children assembled, and in spite of our disturbing presence began their lessons with a wonderful avidity, each section murmuring its individual task *sotto voce*, by which means, I suppose, the mistress, who now seemed more a conductor than a teacher, could be satisfied that all the groups were at work. In the face of such a determined application we felt a trifle frivolous and more in need of some earnest education than the pupils were in need of an entertainment.

In spite of their disposition to learning, the pupils, joined by the neighbours from the farm, tolerated our performance. They were, in fact, a delightful audience to whom we could perform without strain, and without condescension. They laughed and wept with the puppets. We were as one. But it was soon all over ; the children went to their lunch, and we were forced to consider the next step. As the rain was inclined to cease we determined to march on, and after a final meal with our legs under a table we set off from that miraculous hill-top in Wyresdale that had sheltered us so kindly.

We set off, but rather vaguely, and eventually we came to Bay Horse after straggling through Dolphinholme by pleasant ways but without adventure. At Bay Horse we planned to camp so that we could get into Lancaster for letters, and we took the road towards Caton which skirts Lancaster and that frightful main road that carries all the traffic passing north or south. The Caton road mounted the country, and we imagined a delightful camp overlooking the world to Morecambe Bay, but we seemed to hit on all the wrong farms in applying for a camp. By degrees Bay Horse was a thing of the past, and it was in another country altogether that we hit on two old cronies in a field, stalked them round a barn, lost them behind a wall, and eventually waylaid them as they came through a gate. One was the farmer of the land, and he had no objection to our camping. In fact, we were amiably incorporated in their conversation, which was about the water supply on his land. He had just had a water diviner at work, and had dug a well according to the divinations. " Come and look at it," he said, and we all trudged across the field to inspect the new well, to uncover it, and to go down on our knees so that we could peer into its depth. It was quite exciting ; we measured the depth of water with a stick, and, as some of the forked sticks were about which the diviner had used, we grasped them and marched about holding them in the correct position, and hoping that some mysterious force would seize them and wrench them out of our hands. But we must have been very insensitive, or we experimented on a very dry portion of the field, for not one of us obtained the slightest pull in the direction of hidden supplies of water.

"Ah," said one of the old men, "if there wur a barrel o' beer, now, down under, I know one as would be more successful."

My stick, I thought, had a tendency to rise, but what that would indicate I could not conceive. It was probably due to a twist in the wood; or it may have been the water in the sky, which at the moment was climbing up behind the hill in a terrifyingly black mass.

We put up the tent because it looked as if its shelter would soon be necessary, and our two cronies examined everything with an intense and flattering interest. They were a trifle puzzled as to the importance of puppet-showing, and camping was outside their ideals or experience; consequently their tough Lancashire brains put us through a severe catechism. They must first of all be satisfied as to whether we could make it pay—the supreme question in Lancashire. In replying that it did pay we had no idea of their standards or what "making it pay" came to exactly in pounds, shillings, and pence, and we were mean enough not to tell them our earnings. But they took our word for it, and then passed to the question of food. What did we eat? It was now necessary to confess that we were what are called vegetarians.

"Eh? Don't you eat any meat? Then what do

you eat ? Take breakfast, now, if you don't mind me asking ; what would you have for breakfast, like, if you can't take any bacon ? "

" Well, there's coffee or tea, and porridge or cereals, and toast and bread and butter, and marmalade or honey, and fruit and nuts, and eggs—fried, boiled, poached, or scrambled—there's fried tomatoes, mushrooms, taters, rissoles——"

" Ee ! Ba goom ! Ah think ah could do wi' being a vegetarian if you get all that ! And dinner, now, what d'you do abaht dinner ? "

" We eat salads, and cheese and bread and biscuits, and fruit. We sometimes get fruit pies from the baker, and we have these two saucepans, you see, and can cook stews, and macaroni, and rice, and vegetables if we want to."

" Then you do get something t'eat, an' all, then, you do ! And what abaht supper ? "

" Oh, soups, or hot milk, or porridge, or anything that's going and according to what we fancy."

" And what's your idea in not eating any meat, now ? If ah wur you ah should want a bit o' summat t'eat wi' all that walking and pulling. What's your idea, like ? "

We explained cautiously some of our reasons, which were listened to with grave attention.

" Ee ! Ah enjoyed that, didn't you, Tom ? " said one turning to the other.

" Aye, that wur very interesting to me," replied the other. " Ah never 'eard owt like it afore ! "

" Tell us some more. Ah like to 'ear abaht something

new, like. It's interesting, it is. Now, if you don't mind me asking, what d'you do when you—when you—well, if you don't mind me asking, what d'you do, now, when you go to bed ? D'you undress, like ? "

I exhibited pyjamas, and he cast a bashful but pleased glance at them.

" And what d'you do abaht washing ? "

I showed a toilet case, which he looked at more closely.

" And what abaht washing your clothes ? "

" We can do them in this ! " and I showed a canvas basin.

" What ! In that bag ? " and it had to be filled with water to convince him.

" Aye, that's a handy thing, now. Ee ! that is interesting, that is. And d'you sleep wi' the tent open or shoot ? "

Followed a demonstration of how the tent could be open or closed according to circumstances.

" Well, ah think ah'd have it shoot ! And have you got a light ? "

Nothing was left to chance ; they had to be sure that we were provided with everything, and when they could think of no more questions they repeated again their exclamations of, " Ee ! that wur interesting, now," and they hoped we would stay over the next night so that they could come for another chat and learn something more of people who lived an entirely different life from theirs and whose thoughts were apparently so odd that they might have come from another planet.

There was thunder and rain all the evening, but the morning astonished us by being brilliantly fine. We were getting so accustomed to the rainy, the half rainy, the wholly rainy or the damnably rainy that a clear golden morning was almost annoying ; we could scarcely believe in its reality ; it did not belong to us ; it only reminded us of fine weather, of what might be, of sunny weather we had known, and tantalised us like a mirage. And yet we packed and sauntered off, and dawdled along a lovely road pitched high in the country looking over the flats below and away to Lancaster and Morecambe Bay. The fields were green —Lancashire green—very bright against the dark trees, and we hardly pushed the barrow a couple of yards without leaving it to sit and to take this opportunity of enjoying the warm sun without fear of an immediate downpour. We sat on walls, on heaps of stones, on grassy banks among bracken and under trees ; we scrambled into woods and on to hills in meadows where we could stand and see the beautiful Lancashire, and Morecambe Bay gleaming in the west, and the green hills rising over our road eastwards.

After Quernmore, which has one of those sensibly contracted but unspellable pronunciations, we rose again and then fell to a wide green valley, a basin in the hills shut off from the distant views, a rural world in itself of a few farms and much pasturage with a church and a school standing by themselves in the bottom of the grassy bowl. This looked like a performance ; it was obviously our duty to attack this lonely school and to disturb the serenity of its quiet life in the vale. Poor things ! There they were, alone with the works of the gods, the crude surface of the world and the sun, which you could not turn on and off with a tap, the breeze, which no draught protector could shut out, and the songs of the birds that still used their little voices instead of learning to play saxophones. Poor things ! How could they live in this green solitude, with no cotton mill to deafen them and no tall chimney to poison them with its smoke. Unhappy creatures, who must live without the blessings of civilisation ! No crowded traffic to kill them, no tube railways to stifle them, and no cinema to ruin their eyesight. It was obvious that something must be done about it, and, after putting off the good deed as long as possible, we descended on that little school.

It was nervous work introducing ourselves to the school. We entered a small, empty class-room, and tried to screw up our courage to interfere with the proceedings in the larger room. A small girl appeared, was too shy to attend to us as we asked for the teacher, and disappeared again without a word. We followed, pushing ourselves by will power farther into the academy and suddenly encountered the mistress, who had been informed by the girl after all. We at once realised that the school had no awe for the mistress, and that, with her, the human interest came before the scholastic. We very soon learned that there could be no performance as practically the whole school had suddenly gone down with measles. Some half-dozen children were still unspotted, but our own skins began to feel irritable and a strategic retirement seemed

desirable. But having foolish'y admired an exhibition
of craft-work, the boy responsible for the exhibits was
told off to show us his work, and we loitered dangerously
with this youth who might have been casting forth
measles at us all the time. With great care the lad had
constructed from cardboard an admirable farmyard, a
Tudor village, and an aerodrome, but I am afraid that
my thoughts were more on that beastly disease, measles.
Measles ! All those complaints in the plural are particularly loathsome and humiliating. Mumps, rickets, and
adenoids ! We began to edge along the desks to the
door, but again we were stopped. The mistress had
heard about the puppets and some conversation on the
subject was necessary. Then there were the drawings
by one of the boys to look at—Newall—a clever boy of
twelve who drew for the local papers. Very interesting. Most interesting. But a creepy feeling stole
round the roots of our hair, and there was the suspicion
of a catch in the breath as if a latent dry cough was
about to demonstrate. Gradually we emerged into the
sunlight again, and set about putting a good distance
between us and the infected school. We had never
seen a measle, but we could imagine it, and we walked
fast with a tacit understanding, I think, that a little
speed might outwit any of the creatures that happened
to be following. And so we fled from that lovely
serene valley that occasioned such sarcastic thoughts
and whose remote and healthy-seeming airs had suddenly stricken about thirty children within a week.

The road carried us along under woods and by
he lges gay with the wild rose and the white elderberry ;

by farms and meadows and under sharp rising hillsides, until we came out to a lovely scene across the valley of the Lune, where we lingered instead of descending upon Caton with the show. But when we did reach Caton it was to find it threaded with traffic and not inviting to a performance at all, so we walked through, crossed the wide and rushing Lune, and having walked a good way and finding the hill decidedly hard work, we retired into the magnificent Guest House and Youth Hostel, whose handsome stones and gardens overhang a swift bend of the river.

If the Guest House had been full of visitors it would have been a very convenient and delightful place for a performance, but there was nothing to keep us there, and we went on. It was fascinating to be able to walk on and on in a fine evening. There was no money in it, and no sense at all, but it was fascinating. It was slow work. We started ascending, and we went on ascending, extremely steeply, until we came out to the main road to Kirkby Lonsdale, an exhilarating road perched up over the lovely Lune valley and exhibiting to us a tremendous range of hilly country, all the road we had travelled during the day, a bright streak of Morecambe Bay, and a suggestion of Lancaster, round which we had semicircled and were now leaving behind.

Together with this vast expanse of land that lay below us, there was also revealed a greater width of sky, and we were alarmed to see that some very thundery clouds were creeping into the fine evening. A farmer said that his fields were full, and directed us to a gypsy pitch by the side of the road a little farther on.

We hurried up the road and came to the free patch of ground, and while the great cloud piled up we hunted round, like frightened rabbits, for cover. The gypsy pitch was impossible for a tent. There was a litter of old iron and rags that made it disgusting, but fortunately over the wall there was an old quarry in the farm grounds, and as the first thunder rolled we pitched our equipment over the wall, rolled it down the slope, and set up the tent in great haste. We could see the farmer later ; and in the meantime we cowered in the tent, listening to the thunder, which, eventually, produced very little rain with a great deal of noise.

The evening quietened, but we were too tired to tramp over fields to seek the farmer's permission. We were well hidden in the quarry, we were doing no damage, and it was more romantic to pitch a camp and sleep untrammelled with a prosaic permission, and certainly cheaper not to pay any rent. There might, of course, be a bull in the irregular pastures that led off from the quarry, but it was unlikely. We sank deep into our reading and forgot everything.

But what was that ? A small, shrill voice was speaking. " Look, Joe ! What's that ? "

" What is it ? It's something white."

" I dunno. Why—why, it's a tent ! Who is it ? "

We were discovered ! Two boys were peering through the bushes at the quarry edge. Luckily they were much more interested in examining the camp than in the fact that we had settled on their father's land. We hastened to feed them with chocolate, to tell them how much the tent had cost, and to show them our waterproof matchbox, a fascinating gadget. They became very friendly. They assured us that father " wouldn't care a dash."

The boys went and we settled down comfortably for the night, but we could not have been asleep very long before I was awakened by the vague sense of a shadowy something having passed the tent. I sat up and a large animal snorted. Was it the bull ? Risking all, I hit the tent suddenly and loudly. There was a hurried scamper and the departure of a heavy body—evidently not a bull.

It is this succession of unexpected events that sustains this travelling, camping life and keeps one pleasantly alive. In the morning the fun began again very early ; another snorting animal awakened us, a horse this time, and when we had driven him away and were hoping to sleep a little more, a herd of cows came cropping their way into the quarry. There is nothing more disturbing than to have your head on a level with, and within a few paces of, half a dozen chewing cows. They chew all round the tent, tearing off the grass, crunching it noisily. One suddenly coughs in your right ear ; another snorts in your left ; a third, poor thing, utters a hoarse, melancholy sigh, and so they go round your bed, coughing, biting, snorting, sneezing and, of course, stupidly stumbling over a guy-line and nearly wrecking your house. It was more comfortable to get up than to try to snatch another hour's sleep.

The morning was stormy but bright ; it was evident that there had been a storm somewhere in the night, and now large clouds were flying over a brilliant sky.

It was a road on the grand scale, keeping us always in view of romantic hills and odd portions of the bay. The light was fitful and the landscape alive. A hill would disappear in mist and shadow and emerge again ; at one moment it was a deep blue and the next an airy nothing that you could hardly distinguish from the mist ; now it was pale and bright with sunlight, the ghostly colours standing out from a background of black storm-cloud. And the wind blew and blew, tossing the wayside grasses, the gold, the purple, and the white, and bearing with it the scent of honeysuckle and wild rose from the clusters in the hedges.

We lost our way, but did not mind, it was so intoxicating. Somewhere we missed a small road and wandered round until, on the edge of what we imagined to be Green Hill, we discovered that a descent to lower country was necessary to reach Nether Kellet. But we were loath to go down there from the eminence, and we sat and lunched, and sat again, until the brightness went out of the day, and all those variegated hills turned to grey and the view shortened. We went down then to the road by all the lime-kilns and the frequent rocky quarries, like ruined castles, in the fields, to survey Nether Kellett, in which we decided to perform after we had found a camp.

A farmer, working at his hay, let us into a delightful meadow very readily, and on the level turf, sprinkled with daisies, once more we set up our comic home. We were imbibing the necessary tea before returning to the village, when our old friend, the rain, spattered the tent. The farmer and his men, who had almost cleared the hayfield, began to shout and to run, and, joining them in the field, I was recklessly armed with a formidable pitchfork and had the honour of pitching a few last cocks on the last load. Then we raked round the hedges while the horse-rake cleaned up the field, and when it was finished it was both too wet and too late to think about a performance ; but I had helped with the hay, and it is not possible to do that every day of one's life.

Something went wrong with the next day. Probably the wet journey over the Trough had tired us more than we imagined, but we were also discovering a west-country lethargy that made us very weak on that grey day of mizzling rain. Also we had both forgotten to wind watches, and as there was no sun to steer by we went by instinct. We spent the morning writing letters, and after lunch we set off to Lancaster to collect corres-pondence from the post office. As I say, we had steered our way thus far by instinct. It had seemed very easy, and we began to suspect that watches were useless encumbrances, but when we got into Carnforth, just after lunch, we thought all the town clocks had gone mad. They all registered five o'clock. Five o'clock ! Then we must have lunched at four o'clock, and breakfasted at twelve or thereabouts. It was deplor-able, but funny, and we did not care. Everything was crazy on that Carnforth-Lancaster road. Every kind of vehicle was crowded there in a fidgety, untidy, noisy, dirty stream, and, coming to it from a pretty field of clean turf and white daisies, it was perfectly easy to see that the great majority of human beings are certainly crazy. It must be right. It is a conclusion that explains so many human activities. We are crazy.

But, you will say, we were being carried swiftly, conveniently, and marvellously to our letters. Yes, that is true, but a great deal depends upon whether the letters were worth fetching. We had good reason to suppose that none of them contained money ; on the other hand, it was quite likely that there would be bills. Tom would write and say that he was too busy to write, as usual. Mary would write and say, " Isn't the weather awful ? " Jim would—no, Jim would not write at all, but Bill would write saying the weather was filthy. Really, you can hardly argue that ordinary letters are worth risking your life for on a typical main road. We could have had them sent on to a quiet village, but obviously we were crazy. The prevailing epidemic seized us, and we had to have five penn'orth of speed in the local bus.

Lancaster was delightful when we had extricated ourselves from the streets and had climbed the hill with its church and castle, and could look, with hopeful eyes, on those lovely places it was possible to escape to from the town. The waters of Morecambe Bay stretched before us, and beyond was a panorama of the Lake mountains, a wild, tossed-up country, unbelievably bright and blue, looking so clean and pure after the unholy medley of the road, and infinitely attractive. It attracted us. We decided to point the barrow in that direction when we moved again.

It was restful on the Castle Hill. It was all composure and art up there, with its cobbled ways, the discreet

147

eighteenth-century houses, the castle itself and the parish church. It had all been beastly enough at one time or another. Nowhere could a lurid fiction-writer for dear little boys find better material for stories of heroic murderings, spirited plunderings, pious arson, and lawful cruelties. But the ambitious rulers and the destructive soldiers have departed, and peace and thoughtfulness remain with the craftsmanship of workmen and the compositions of artists.

Above all there are the fourteen canopied stalls in the chancel of the church. They stand there, those old carved wooden seats, cut off from everything else by their beauty. We were stumbling round without guide or knowledge, trusting to our taste and inclinations, and a trifle bored, but we came to a stop and woke up before the gracious elegance of those stalls. Here was expressed in carved wood, as in any work of art, all the subtle human consciousness of the sensitive balance of life, its infinite intricacy and interdependence of every part with the other. It was all there in the twists and turns, the light and shade, the design, and in the cuts of the chisels, all combining to an instant effect of harmless loveliness. They stood, as they have stood for six hundred years, like sentient beings beneath a spell of all-knowing inspiration, and I can see them still, standing clear above all else in Lancaster, those fourteen spires of carved wood dreaming of loveliness in the church on the Castle Hill.

So that was Lancaster, and it was enough for us. We came away with letters and shopping, and were amusingly given a lift in a car that had been carrying a bride and a bridegroom and wedding guests, and was cheerfully littered with confetti. The driver was cheerful, too, and overflowing with the milk of human kindness. He dropped us at the gate in the lane very unwillingly, being entirely incredulous that we could be camping in the field.

The tent was waiting for us entirely unmolested, as usual, and in the delightful meadow we subsided to serenity, studying the maps and choosing a road that would take us towards that blue line of mountains we had seen over the bay from Castle Hill.

XV

WARTON AND THE YEALANDS

A VERY red dawn encouraged us to pack quickly. "Red morning, shepherd's warning," runs the old adage, and it is about the only one that seems to have any sense in it. So we hoped to get through a dry packing, and then to wobble on foolishly and shape our day according to the amount of water that would probably distribute itself very freely over us and the hay lying in the fields. If the dawn was not encouraging to us frivolous showmen, it must have been still less so to the farmers, who were in the thick of hay-making and had their crops about in the fields, some lying in swathes, some tossed up, and some in cocks ready for carrying. One day's rain would undo a great deal of hard work, if it did not actually ruin the hay, and one could imagine the farmers all round, in various stages of undress, sticking their heads out of bedroom windows, stumping round the yards in unlaced boots, and scowling at the red dawn. Swearing, too, I should think.

It perhaps explained the mood at our farm when we called to render thanks for being allowed to camp. "That's all right. Good morning," said the mistress, turning her back and walking away in the middle of my speech. It may have been the weather, but it may have

been Lancashire that began to feel prickly and uncomfortable at being thanked politely. The mistress was
probably getting on with the work, saying to herself,
" Don't be so soft ! " and extremely annoyed at being
interrupted with anything so unimportant as thanks.

We were soon walking through Over Kellett, which
turned out to be a handsome village, a real village with
a cross on the green, and numbers of dark, decorative
sycamore trees rising over the stone cottages that had
seventeenth- and eighteenth-century dates carved over
the doors. There was no sign of inhabitants as we
walked across the green and descended, under more
sycamores, the road towards Warton. A brightness
was stealing into the morning, and the hayfields, light
coloured with the drying grass, glittered under the
dark sycamores. The air was heavily burdened with
the scent of hay, and it was a delightful road, descending easily all the time, carrying us calmly through the
beautiful country. Apparently the red dawn had made
a mistake this time.

It was a morning we shall not forget, a still morning
with the sun stealing through the mist. It was summer
in the north of England, with the stone walls between
the fields, the separate, concise, and firmly designed
trees, and a suggestion of rugged topped hills ahead.
There is a clean, simplified shape in the northern
country as if the indifferent and untidy weeds and the
soft, mushy growths get no encouragement there. It
is all clean sweeps of green marked with the strong,
handsome trees, and a suspicion of hard, grey rock
being not far away. The sun grew stronger and the

road prettier. The grass by the road was bright with white clover and the blue crane's-bill; over the walls men were making hay, cows chewing the cud, and sheep grazing peacefully, composing themselves into bright groups on the green grass. We walked lazily. We descended to jingling.

> Of all the roads in England,
>   The one for this fine day,
> Is the road we now are walking
>   Among the fields of hay.
>
> Of all the jobs in England,
>   Just walking is the best;
> You simply shift your feet along—
>   The world does all the rest.
>
> Of all the crimes in England,
>   Hard work's an awful sin;
> The lilies of the field, you know,
>   They neither toil nor spin.
>
> Of all the beasts that flourish,
>   I'd rather be a cow;
> She has the art of lazing,
>   She certainly knows how.

Well, we could not help it. The sun was so hot and we travelled at so many yards an hour, rather than miles. This road, we knew, could not go on for ever and we made the most of it. The uncut meadows were rich and green with the clover, and the white flowers were bright in the sward. The cattle put their heads against tree trunks and swished their tails rhythmically to combat the flies. A light breeze rustled the leaves ; someone was singing in the distance. Here there was a clear beck by the road and there we passed over a canal bridge, the idle beasts standing in the lazy water, and the tall reeds in the shallows swaying with graceful, idle ease. In one meadow a solitary man loitered, looking for mushrooms ; here a farmer at a gate slowly searched his coat, found a cigarette, hunted lazily for matches, gave us a comfortable good day, lit up, and gazed dreamily round the sunny, misty fields. Man seemed to be in his proper proportion here, something smaller than the great earth, and not a pert creature talking condescendingly about the country. And he was not a marketing board uttering vulgarities about sales. He stood, letting nature do its work, and then skilfully and artfully stepped in at just the right time to seize his crop of hay. A small creature, making a cunning use of an infinitesimal speck of the universe.

We turned west by Borwick Hall, the old mansion in which Fuller Maitland, the music critic, lived and collected ancient instruments. He ought to have been a musician, for that clear country had all the lovely order and firm calculations of Bach. We heard, too, of old marionettes being there. Someone had seen them at the bottom of a cupboard, tumbled in a heap, and our thoughts went out to those ancient comrades who were no longer on the road, whose threads were hopelessly tangled so that they could dance no more. We feared

153

this was the end of the idyllic morning, for we were approaching the main road out of Carnforth ; but when we had crossed it with care, we found our quiet road again, going up the hill to Warton, mounting the opposite side of the valley we had been travelling, mounting towards the high grey rocks of Warton Crag.

The shape of the village was not inviting to a performance and we went to the school, but the head master being at his lunch we had the pleasure of tracking him down at his house. He was very undisturbed by the barrow pulling up before his elegant villa, and could see at once the educational value of a puppet performance in the school, if not in the performance itself, at least in the good humour and pleasant feeling it would bring into the school and so prepare the ground for better things. He spoke of his pupils as if they were all his children and he an indulgent parent, and it lent an added charm to the pleasant day to hear him say that he found not only attention in them, but affection as well.

We were to introduce the puppets to this delightful academy after the afternoon lessons, and in the meantime we hoisted the tent in the small back garden of an empty house. There was barbed wire all round us, like a concentration camp, and some tenants of the adjoining house to overlook this Wild West activity in the neighbouring garden. But we were greatly compensated by having the key of the empty house, and as the fine day suggested some thunder later on it was reassuring to have this refuge behind us.

The affectionate scholars seemed a very intelligent audience at the time, and regaled us with tremendous applause, but we were not so sure later, when we heard that one child had run into his house after the show, and cried, " Muther ! There's been a man at the school acting daft ! " But we enjoyed the performance in the village school, and it was an altogether appropriate ending to this lovely day, one of the few summer-looking, hay-making days of the summer. But, of course, it must rain in the evening, not that we minded, for it was pleasant enough to sit in the tent and look through the barbed wire up to Warton Crag. We should have been inspecting the village church to find the arms of George Washington's family, that lived in Warton for three hundred years. But it was too wet, and instead we speculated as to whether the removal of the Washington family from Lancashire to America had been so good for them that George had come into being in all his magnificence ; or if, had they remained in Warton, would George have never heard of that cherry tree. A futile question, but we were tired with a long day, and rolling up in the sleeping-bags we fell asleep in the back garden and did not awake until I found myself sitting up suddenly with instinctive awareness. A man, with a handkerchief of mushrooms in his hand, was leaning over the wire fence, peering into our tent—our bed-chamber.

" What are you looking at ? " I shouted angrily and uselessly.

" Ah was only looking to see if there was anyone in ! " he mumbled lamely, and shambled off. If only he had remained we might have asked if he was in the habit of looking into other people's bedrooms to see if anyone was in, or what he had intended to do if there had been no one in. But you are never safe from people who will look upon a tent as a public spectacle, and will blunder in on your privacy as they would never think of doing in a house.

Warton and the fine day was the entrance to a magic world, and on that hill-side under Warton Crag we walked through deep woods in an entirely new country. Sheltered by the Furness peninsula, and on the borders of the western sea there is a soft air and a more luxuriant growth. It is the way into a quiet, green hill-country of old villages and grey-stone farms, looking out over the valley and the hills eastwards, and over Morecambe Bay and the Westmorland mountains to the west. Added to the soft air was a particularly muggy day with a warm rain falling. We became entirely unstuck, as if the glue between our joints had melted, and after two miles of slothful progress under the trees among the birds and squirrels we longed to set up the tent in those leafy woods and give ourselves up to languid idleness. And in this magic world our desires were granted. We came to a stop at the village with the romantic name of Yealand Conyers.

It was Yealand Manor that pandered to this ignoble mood. The Society of Friends have recently acquired this house and estate which is being developed as a Guest House, and there could be no more appropriate managers of this estate, for outside the entrance gates stands an old meeting-house ; the whole district is rich in Quaker tradition, one of those remarkable early Friends, Richard Hubberthorne, being a Yealand man, and it is of this village that George Fox writes in his journal : " After I was recovered, I went to Yelland, where there was a great meeting. In the evening there came a priest to the house, with a pistol in his hand, under pretence to light a pipe of tobacco. The maid of the house seeing the pistol, told her master, who, clapping his hands on the door-post, told him he should not come in there. While he stood there, keeping the door-way, he looked up, and spied over the wall a company of men coming, some armed with staves, and one with a musket. But the Lord God prevented their bloody design ; so that seeing themselves discovered, they went their way, and did no harm."

We approached the house by the long drive through the park with the feeling that we were very appropriate visitors. In this manner, in the old days, wandering Punch and Judy men must have visited the great country houses, always sure of a large Victorian family to be amused in those days before parents were so cruel as to turn their children out of hearth and home to be looked after in mobs by strange men and women. We tried to imagine sixteen eager children's faces watching our approach from the schoolroom window, while Charlotte Brontë, as the governess, stood behind, restraining their excited cries to a more genteel decorum. " It is Professor Wilkinson," we imagined her saying, " a truly respectable man who travels with his wife, a much-respected person. They are an estimable couple, and we will ask Mamma's permission for them to exhibit their quaint old performance, which was always such a source of amusement, as is widely known, to the great Dr. Johnson."

By this time we were at the house and in a very few minutes the kind warden had fallen in with our plans. Walking was over for the day ; we were going to be idle and languid. There was to be a performance, and we were introduced to the rabbit meadow behind the house where we could camp. More than a meadow, it was half a mile of glade between handsome woods, a ravishing, wild, retired length of green with a huge amphitheatre in its centre. As the warden remarked, you could not look at it without thinking of pageants. And here, between the woods and in company with hundreds of rabbits, we put the tent.

It was the first thoroughly undomesticated camp of the summer. There was not a house to be seen, not even a chicken-house or a cow-house, and no barbed wire. It was wild, uncultivated ground, and with every step there rose a scent of herbs, while little wild flowers were in the grass and purple thistles and tansy waved above them all. We were enclosed by nut bushes and by the trees of the woods on either side, in which you imagined badgers and foxes and out of which came hundreds of rabbits, numbers of which added to the enchantment by being black, and some miraculously white. We were safe from the wicked world, and as the hours went by and the shadows crept into one long side of the glade we expected to see hobgoblins join the white rabbits, and fairies sneak out timidly, in spite of the twentieth century, and dance a few defiant turns. They were possibly there all the time, but we had not the eyes to see them.

Idle as we were before, we now relaxed still further, shed shoes and socks and all unnecessary garments, and loafed as Adam must have loafed in Eden. There was some lazy rain, some warm sun, a little idle thunder in the distance, and the warm, western air sapped us of all ambition and wicked energy. We thought of doing this and spoke of doing that, but we did exactly nothing, except slowly to order our camp, spread our beds, and drink tea without milk because we were too lazy to fetch it.

To give a performance was disturbing until the time came to do it, and then it was a pleasure to set up the theatre in the playroom of the house, with the french windows opening out to flowers and to the park beyond. A good-looking audience of guests, staff, and village behaved themselves remarkably well before the puppets, laughed at most of the right places, applauded at the right times, and altogether gave us a pleasurable evening ; and, not content with that, they fed us and sent us away heavy with a collection of silver coins— not a brown 'un among them !

After that we relapsed again very contentedly into doing nothing but wander about the immediate neighbourhood. Behind the tent was a path that traced a worn line in the grass under the nut bushes, through a gate, and into a second wilderness of turf and bracken and rocks. It rambled on over grassy bumps, into little dells and eventually climbed its way over grey rocks till we came out clear above the bushes and trees and were astonished to see all Morecambe Bay before us, and again the Lake mountains, nearer, more formidable, but yet over the water and all massed together in their own distant world, a blue, wild country just beneath the clouds. We stood in Lancashire and could see most of Westmorland, with a foreground of falling woods, green, luxurious farms, and the waters of the bay running inland to the foot of the hills like a lake.

We staggered to the village and collected letters from the cottage post office, and wandered down the hill between the old houses and farms, bought some home-made butter and milk at last, and climbed the hill again to Elizabeth Brockbank's studio, to see her paintings and the original drawings of her books about the district, drawings of farmers, and cloggers, the retired sailor, anglers, and the man who used to play a species of zither for the country dances. There were pictures, too, of the surrounding houses, of interiors with enormous fireplaces, and rugged beams, and built-in cupboards, settles, and chests, any one of which would have provided sufficient timber for a row of modern houses. There were also drawings by the villagers, for Miss Brockbank keeps an open studio for anyone who is bold enough to sit down and draw, and as for the gardener of the Manor, he cuts Miss Brockbank's wood engravings professionally, and had, that morning, started making a puppet-show before breakfast.

A delightful village, Yealand Conyers, one of the best, with its steep road on the hill-side, its trees and dignified houses, and the ravishing view over the plains and the hills from the head of the village. It was with a shock one remembered that it was in Lancashire, that Lancaster was but a few miles away, and then Preston and all that world of tall chimneys. One reads of thoughtful conferences debating their affairs at Blackpool ; they would have more room to think and to concentrate at Yealand. If all the serious bodies of Oldham, Bolton, Wigan, Blackburn and the like could confer in those Manor grounds for a few days, a serenity would come down on them, and a beauty surround them that would impart subtle information as to " the shape of things to come." Yealand caught us in a dangerous mood, and we were more inclined to stay there for ever than for two days. Particularly when we returned to the tent to find a heap of fresh vegetables from the kitchen garden and a large pot from the kitchen.

And yet we moved on, packing under a dangerous sky which now seemed to be a fixed condition of the journey. We had simply given up all preconceived notions as to what ought to happen, and we just went staggering on, extracting what pleasure, education, and moral improvement we could from the unfortunate circumstances. One always thinks of " life on the open road " and puppet-shows out of doors as being enacted, like Utopias, in perpetual sunlight. Given fine weather you can put your heart into it, but under a perpetual dictatorship of rain the thing becomes a grim farce. There seemed little sense in moving from a dry pitch, but we pulled out of that fairy glade and had got as far as the post office, half-way through the village, when there seemed still less sense. The sky was unchanged ; it was the same close, loose-looking vapour, but suddenly the largest sized drops began to tumble out of it. The drops were joined by lumps of hail, and, jumping over the river in the gutter which had formed in about two minutes, we sheltered in the post office. The deluge did not last any length of time, but long enough to flood a few hayfields, batten down a good many acres of oats, disturb numbers of outdoor fêtes and bazaars, and give us cause to wonder what would happen next.

With the cessation we pushed on, and cleared the next small village of Yealand Redmayne with its lovely old stone houses perched high above the country, and as there was every promise of more cloudbursts we began to make up our minds. There were two roads before us ; with good weather we could go on through Beetham and Milnthorpe and stroll round the estuary into Cartmel, but with this unpromising demonstration of what the sky can do we were more inclined to branch off to Arnside, where we knew we could get shelter indoors. It was not long before we decided quite definitely. We pulled up a stiff hill in suffocating heat and in a queer nightmarish light. There was a crash of thunder, an equal crash of rain, and we were caught with no sign of shelter. We looked through one hedge for a farm ; there was nothing. We peered through the other to see only the deserted fields. Before us the road turned a corner and we ran, hoping for hidden shelter there. The thunder crashed and the rain hissed, roared, and danced on the road ; it rained as impossibly as one has seen it in a storm drama at the cinema ; it was so thick that it brought an appreciable pressure on the head and shoulders ; you could feel the heavy, separate drops striking your shoes. We streamed with the deluge and our eyes were flooded with water. In a moment the world was cold, and our clothes penetrated with chilly patches. We decided to go to Arnside and get indoors.

It must have been a mile before we came to a farm with a deep archway leading to the yard, and, although the inclined ground under it was a stream, we piloted the barrow under the arch in a rapid and graceful curve. It was draughty, but we were able to shake off some of the water and hang our coats up to drain. We lunched on Yealand Manor scones and a variety of nonsense out of the hamper. We did not mind in what absurd order we ate cheese and chocolate—we were out of the rain, and were going to Arnside to get inside a house for the week-end at least.

XVI

DIGRESSION IN THE RAIN:
GRANGE, CARTMEL, CONISTON

" THE weather conditions of late have been far
from in keeping with what would naturally be
expected in July."—*Local Press*.

In other words, the weather was foul. Being near the
mountains the possibility of rain was to be expected,
but this summer it was not a local peculiarity but a
national calamity ; a calamity, at least, for all organ-
isers of outdoor activities. I do not speak for manu-
facturers of umbrellas and raincoats, or for ducks, or
for those amateurs with rain gauges on their lawns.
They must have been very, very happy. But for
farmers, for coco-nut shies, for Punch-and-Judies, and
for campers the summer was a wash-out ; it was
diluted beer ; it was watered milk ; it was another
destroying Flood.

The scene at Arnside opens with us breakfasting in
bed, while the barrow was housed in a farm shed down
the hill, waiting in readiness if the waters should
suddenly go down. They did not look like going down
and we did not look like getting up, for some time. A
watery mist blotted out the scene, and coffee from an
electric stove drowned our cares. Over the hills and
the estuary the grey veils of water joined the earth and

164

sea and the low sky in one absurdity of general damp-
ness that nothing dressed in clothes could live in.
With the animals it was different. From our room we
looked out on to sheep and cows, and these extraordinary animals reclined gracefully and contentedly
in the wet grass, letting the rain sweep over them while
they chewed the grass as if it was all extremely pleasant.
Perhaps it was—for them. Perhaps it would be for us
if we could rid ourselves of the dictatorship of clothing
and have sufficient pride to enjoy our own hair instead
of the growths of inferior animals. Clothing is absurd.
We wear socks to keep our feet warm, but only a hero
dare walk without socks if the temperature is at boiling-
point. Without clothes we might have gone on pushing
the barrow through the rain without a thought except
to say, " How refreshing is the rain after all that sun !
I do like a thoroughly wet day sometimes ! Isn't this
rain lovely ! " Actually the fault lay with those restless ancestors of ours who colonised this island, this
isolated piece of mud with the uncertain climate of mist,
fog and rain, which seemed at times to be attached to the
world of clouds. As a matter of fact, in spite of ancestors
and clothes we were tolerably content for the time
being. A house is never so interesting as when you
have been without one for a time. After the confine-
ment of the tent it was an extraordinary pleasure just to
walk across the room, to feel the firm boards and dry
rugs under your toes, and to look out of the window at
the descending sheets of rain.

But we did get up and walk out to look at Arnside,
and discovered many little gardens packed with bright

flowers and with large fuchsias and fig trees which seem to go with a mild climate. There were even roses planted in the streets by the voluntary efforts of the citizens, and I hope they will go on doing that, as nothing could be more sensational than to have a holiday town all one flower garden. We went on down the hill under the trees and found a small, innocent promenade, a long view down the estuary, and that caterpillar-like railway bridge over the sands, leading to Grange and to all that "Lancashire north of the sands," which, at the moment, was under a cloud. And it was not long before the rain was splashing round us, and we were forced indoors again, to read the novels of Constance Home, and to laugh at "the weather conditions which of late have been far from in keeping with what would naturally be expected in July."

A second attempt to explore Arnside carried us farther. We got to some fields behind the town, and wandered among the stone walls, the ferns and mosses, and the wild flowers in search of the *Fairy Steps*, and penetrated a hinterland of pleasant farms. The path took us into a wood with a weird groundwork of rocks split into frequent chasms, in the cool depths of which a variety of ferns were flourishing. The path mounted among the nut bushes towards a wall of rock, and we walked up a narrow split to the summit imagining that we had achieved the *Fairy Steps*. But this is doubtful, as a cloud swept over us and obliterated any further vision, and trusting to our sense of direction we wandered off along the hill, waded through clumps of dripping bracken, climbed walls, and slushed through

166

long grass until we fell over yet one more wall into a road. The mist changed to rain and we could see this delightful country behind Arnside, the quiet grassy fells, the roads running between stone walls, and masses of crane's-bill growing in the verge. And turning towards Arnside we had before us The Knott, that hill which *is* Arnside, a steep, wooded fell rising suddenly from the meadows with dramatic effect.

With a sudden clearance in the late evening we made a third attempt to master the beauties of Arnside by climbing The Knott. We walked some genteel paths among the seats on the slopes and were enthusiastic, but it was in climbing a steeper path to the very summit of that natural tower that the full appreciation came to us, not only of the hill itself but of Arnside. There were places on that path where we looked under pine trees to a fairy panorama of the sandy estuary running up to the green fields and woods at its head. Above the fields were the rounded hills, now grey in the rain, now blue in the shadow, and then emerald green in the sun ; and behind the low hills rose bigger hills in varied gradation to the blue background of higher peaks, to Coniston Old Man, Skiddaw, the Langdale Pikes, Helvellyn, Sunday Crag and all the rest ; an immense line of craggy points, appearing and disappearing in the clouds, a comprehensive sight of the Lakes which all should see before penetrating those intricate regions. The very summit of The Knott is wild with its storm-tossed trees, and from its edge we looked over all Morecambe Bay from Silverdale among its trees below, away to Lancaster on the one side and to misty shores on the other. It was a satisfactory conclusion to the day, and Arnside in three acts and one change of costume had given us a pastoral symphony with a dramatic finale.

The weather conditions et cetera continued, and we began to fidget inside the house whether those conditions were far from in keeping with what would naturally be expected in July or not. At all events we had not come to Lancashire expecting to be tied up in a mere house and, seizing our coats, we went through the rain, not to the barrow, but to the railway station. The weather was a nuisance and it had ruined our project for the time being, but once we had accepted the inevitable reverse to our fortunes the rain ceased to be so significant. We looked upon it quite favourably, for it presented us with a holiday, and instead of maintaining our role of eccentrics against a puzzled world, we could now move through the rain easily and unself-consciously.

The train rumbled us over the long bridge across the sands of the estuary to Grange. The bridge is an ugly affair occasioned by all the ugly industry of Barrow, but it is considerably dwarfed by the immense scene in which it stands, and the trains become toy trains as they puff over the wide sands.

The Sands !

" That's a nasty looking piece," said a youth in the train, indicating a puffy, muddy rise in the miniature desert. " That looks bad, that does ! "

We all looked sagely at the suspected patch without knowing anything about it, but " the sands " are a topic here, and we were grateful to the young man for making our flesh creep. It lifted the train journey into an adventure ; if the train at that moment had tipped us over we would have fallen on " the nasty looking piece " ; we imagined ourselves struggling in the quicksand ; we were pleasantly relieved when it was passed.

Less than a hundred years ago, if we had wanted to get into this " Lancashire north of the sands," it would have been necessary to push the barrow across the seven-mile sandy waste between Hest Bank, near Lancaster, to Kents Bank, just south of Grange. It was the quickest route north and was in constant use. From Arnside it had been possible to see in the distance, daily, a diminutive procession of coaches and riders straggling across this local Sahara. It was an adventurous journey, and in the graveyard of Cartmel Priory are buried over two hundred victims of this amazing passage. The returning tide could rush in on you suddenly ; there were quicksands, and two river channels to ford ; there was the possibility of a fog enclosing you within a few yards of sandy space and robbing you of all sense of direction. There were guides appointed to mark out a route, but accidents would happen, and there were tales of horses and carts disappearing, of a party of young people returning from Lancaster fair and being caught by the tide, or a drunken man setting out and not being seen again. An acquaintance told us of an old family letter in which the writer gave a description of riding across the sands and actually coming upon a traveller sinking in a quicksand. The writer threw out his reins, but was horrified to find that they were not long enough, and while thinking what to do the man disappeared from sight. A gentle gossip goes up about this dangerous old road over the sands. You know—dear me, wasn't travelling dangerous in the old days—but, good gracious, that is nothing to what we can do on quite an ordinary road nowadays! The guides still receive the yearly stipend, I believe, but it is curious that no one seems to indulge in the sport in these days, and yet it would make an excellent " dirt track," or a test run for motor cycles.

Grange has been clever to pitch its station just outside the town, so that you walk into gardens, and then are cheered up by discovering the shops, and finally pass on to the higher and grander district, which shows you the snug position of this small and neat resort under the hills and overlooking the bay. Unfortunately we had noticed in a guide-book that Grange caters for the " wealthy and æsthetic only," and as we might be included in the one, but were most certainly not in the other, and as the weather conditions et cetera were only conducive to indoor life, we mounted a bus for shelter, and allowed it to carry us away. After winding about through many outlying houses and the villages of Cark and Flookborough, we came into the little square of Cartmel, which looked promising, and fetched us out of the bus.

Cartmel square is like a scene in a play. It has an old stone cross, a pump, a mysterious stone table and the old Priory gateway, in the room over which there was a school until one hundred and fifty years ago. The houses are all distinguished, one having an elegantly pillared porch and another a flight of outside stone steps ; there are courts to look into, and the arch of the gateway to look under ; it would be a perfect pitch for a travelling theatre if it were not for the rain, the tourists' cars parked there, and the gyrations of arriving and departing buses.

We passed on to inflict our attentions on the aged Priory Church and to make ourselves feel small and pampered beneath the rough beauty of those rugged stones, so large, so naked and unashamed. Only a few minutes before we had been in a gimcrack, smelly bus, and the transition from that common accumulation of stinks and noise and grease to this work of our unscientific ancestors was a little difficult. It was so devastatingly beautiful that it came down on one like a blow, and wiped out, in a moment, the whole dirty mess of our industrial era. You began to think that it would be better to worship the gods than to manufacture an infinite number of pots and pans ; to build temples rather than factories, and to set up men of learning and culture rather than energetic commercial travellers to manage the world for us.

We moved over to learn something of the edifice from the guide, who was exhibiting the misericords to a group in the choir, but our feelings of awe and admiration were rather disturbed, and we listened in a mixture of irritation and risibility.

" These are the misericords," said the guide. " Here is one of the mermaid . . ."

" Where does the bishop sit when he's here ? "
inquired a Scottish voice, breaking into the story. The
guide explained politely, and continued to describe the
seats again patiently, but again the Scots voice broke
in :

" Have you told them about the guide across the
Morecambe Sands, yet ? "

GUIDE : No ! There isn't much to say about that—
that was a long time ago.

SCOT (*to girl in party*) : Never mind. If you want to
cross the sands the guide's obliged to take you. He
can't refuse, you see. What's he get for doing it ?

GUIDE : Well, I think a small holding. . . . Here
is another beautiful piece of carving—you will see the
vine.

SCOT : Doesn't he get forty-five pounds, left by the
monks ?

GUIDE : This is perhaps the most beautiful of all
the misericords, but on the other side there is a
unicorn.

SCOT : Does he go across on a horse, or what ?

For some time the guide was able to get on with his
talk about the seats, but a new subject started the
interrupter again.

GUIDE : There is the dormer window through
which the monks used to come for matins at two
o'clock.

SCOT : Must have been good men—those——

GUIDE : That is hardly for us to know. . . .

SCOT : Is there fishing hereabouts ?

GUIDE : Yes, there's a small river.

SCOT : Hum ! The monks always built where there were fish. Ever caught any ?

ANOTHER : Tiddlers !

GUIDE : There were trout in it. Here you see the tomb of . . .

SCOT : Did you ever catch a trout ?

GUIDE : No ! But I once caught a pike when I was a boy.

SCOT (*clapping him on the back*) : Guid chap ! Guid chap !

Here there was a straying away on the part of some of the group, but the interrupter would not allow this, although the cause of it, and shouted in a loud voice :

" Now, come on ! Come on ! You've got to see this," and he remarked upon the likeness of Lord Frederick Cavendish, whose tomb is there, to the late King George V.

GUIDE : And that is the banner of Sir Evan Macgregor, who . . .

SCOT : And what connection had the Macgregors with this edifice ?

GUIDE : They settled here. . . .

SCOT : Have they given much to the church ? Are they a charitable family ?

GUIDE : Yes, very kind, I think.

SCOT : Guid ! Very guid ! I like to hear of my own countryfolk giving something away !

GUIDE : . . . the meaning of the word " gree " is step. The charge for burial below the gree was two shillings, and for above the gree three shillings and sixpence. There was no charge for outside. It was free.

SCOT : Guid ! Very guid ! We're all equal in death—three and sixpence'll no make you different !

We left the Priory Church with the usual feeling in leaving such places, that we had not given sufficient time and respect to it, that its grand air did wipe out such a lot of contemporary fussiness and vulgarity, and that one ought to do something more than just look at it, and then go off and eat buns in a tea-shop. But it is what we did, and finding Cartmel relapsing more and more into the ancient days as the evening advanced we thought it would be pleasant to stay the night there. Who knows but what a ghost or two might not walk across that old square in the night, or Cartmel be forgotten on the next day, as it must have been forgotten and remote in the days before the Furness railway, when its church was roofless, its stalls open to the rain, and there was no Grange to send tourists to it.

The small hotel at the end of the square was a proper lodging ; on entering you immediately became intimate with the ceiling, lost the way among the corners and odd steps, and you could almost touch the heads of the passers-by in the street from the bedroom window. The personnel was easy and unobtrusive, and within those walls you are not cut off from the little Cartmel. We were fed decently and simply and walked out to smell the evening air. The rain had ceased and a wild war was going on in the heavens between the blue and the grey. Hampsfell, the famous hill between Grange and Cartmel, was calling to us, and we walked towards it hoping that the sky would permit us to get some way up the attractive slopes. We crossed the fields, passed round the farm, and began to climb under an ominous cloud that slowly drifted across our heads. Slowly it cleared the hill without condensing a drop and, of course, we climbed through the bracken to the very top of Hampsfell.

If the tidiness and respectability of Grange was ordinary, you could not say the same of its wonderful hill, Hampsfell. A broad grassy path led along the ridge of this high fell and led us over miniature cliffs until we arrived at the stone tower on the highest point. And all the time there was Morecambe Bay to one side, and again that tumbled line of the Lake mountains to the other. Immediately below stretched out the treacherous sands, and at our feet were the houses of Flookborough and Cark and the spurs of land running out to the sea. And westwards the Cartmel valley, sheltered by the hill itself, a green valley studded with trees and good grey-stone farms, ran up to the hills, and that evening it was all a weird greeny-grey in the shadow of the storm clouds. Over the valley rose the Coniston mounts, the rain streaking down on their huge forms, which were a deep blue-black, and as flat as cardboard. An orange streak glinted behind the blue-black, and in a moment we had before us the awful beauty and exhilaration and danger of life.

We climbed the little tower, known as the Hospice, and we went inside, where, in spite of the door being missing, we were relieved to see we could get some shelter if one of those blowzy clouds collapsed on its way over the hill. The door was missing and the windows had been blocked permanently with sheets of

metal. There had been an attempt to pitch rubbish
into the fireplace, but a good many people had failed in
their aim. Evidently the cynical notice on the wall had
created some respect, in spite of the door having disappeared.

"All persons visiting this Hospice by permission of
the owner, are requested to respect private property
and not by act of wanton mischief and destruction
show that they possess more muscle than brain. I
have no great hope that this reasonable hope will be
attended to, for as Solomon says : 'Though thou
shouldest bray a fool in a mortar among wheat with
a pestle, yet will not his foolishness depart from him.'"

We swept up the cigarette and chocolate packets with
a bracken brush and started a fire, and also invented a
nice state office for somebody. It would be a good job
for one of our impecunious landscape poets, to be armed
with a besom and a small salary and sent off to climb
all these beauty spots in the kingdom and clean them
up from time to time. To climb all manner of glorious
hills, to sweep a bit and to sonnet a bit, and to make
glorious bonfires of the rubbish of the vulgar, what more
could a poet want !

It was wild on the top of Hampsfell, surrounded by
the great hills and the sea, and so near the swirling sky.
It would have been exciting to pitch the tent there, but
it might have been the end of the tent. Nothing but
stone and the short shrubs could live there. We
scrambled up a rough little cliff thrusting through the

grass and were confronted with a bare tableland of white rock, a queer pavement of limestone carved rhythmically into channels by ages of rain, and split into fissures, deep, cool grottoes in which the hart's-tongue fern miraculously spread its smooth and perfect leaves. It might have been the ruined pavement of an ancient temple ; it was the bleached bones of prehistoric monsters ; was it a dead, desiccated desert or a petrified sea ? It was the old bald-headed top of Hamspfell that had been battered by æons of storms, that must have been the same for the monks of Cartmel eight hundred years ago as for the Ancient Britons, and for any wandering dinosaur that was fool enough to climb it and stretch his long neck there in the unmeasured years before. And one may still walk those primitive slopes ; anyone in Grange can climb the hill with ease, but, curiously, we were alone. There was not another figure to be seen on that exciting hill. It is the one free and magnificent " amusement " for any visitor to that bit of coast—but it was deserted.

The barrow and the puppets were far away, but the weather was disordered and there seemed little use in going back for them. In an optimistic mood we had given Ulverston as a postal address, imagining that we could have strolled there in a few days, but the weather made the possibility of impromptu outdoor performances very remote, and had severely handicapped the nobility of the camping procedure. We had engaged ourselves to perform in Wigton in a few days, and for this we had arranged to take off from Kendal by rail.

In short, we left Cartmel by bus to pick up letters from Ulverston.

Even during the transit by vehicle it was possible to see that this road, running round the estuary of the river Leven, was entirely delightful and, above all, it was an original little world ; it had its own make-up of small hills and valleys, of colour and thick verdure. It would have suited us, with the puppets and the tent. There are small villages and hamlets in which a friendly show might have been knocked up, and there are all sorts of quiet, green corners into which a tent would have fitted comfortably. It is a quiet, green, wild country of bracken and heather hills and the road running through the flat country on the edge of the estuary, under woods and among flat watery pieces, with herons standing about in the undisturbed acres of marshy greenery. It is wild, yet civilised and cultivated. Frequent cottages, with flowers in bits of gardens and ferns in the stone walling, snuggle into retired corners, and an occasional shy residence shows a gate on the road or a chimney-pot among the trees. It should be a place for anglers with the swift river coming down from the hills to the waters of the estuary. It was pleasant in the rain which sprinkled the greenery gently and seemed its natural accompaniment.

We were suddenly tipped into Ulverston, but the very modern post office in the old town had nothing for us. We would have to wait, and there was so much we might do in the meantime that we agitated between north and south, trembled on the verge of going to Furness Abbey, considered Swarthmore, Bardsea and the coast, had not the slightest inclination to Barrow, and were finally captured by a bus labelled Coniston.

The bus was, oh ! so very efficient. It hurried us over the most lovely places as if they were so much dirt, and had us in Coniston almost before it had been possible to read the entrancing advertisements on the bus ticket. And if we had not scrambled out quickly it would have had us in Ambleside in a few more minutes. We had glimpses of the road as we rattled along between the ferny walls, the rocky fields and the woods, and all the stony farms and cottages on the hills. And then it must be delightful when the road joins the lake and rises and falls through the woods by the water's edge, touching the lake at times and then turning into the meadows. But it is a road to loiter on, to live on with a tent for a few days, or to settle on for a year or so, or for a lifetime. If only the weather would improve we would pull the barrow along it yet.

So ! this was Coniston. The local industry appeared to be the providing of endless teas. We all like our tea, of course, but it is a pity that there should be so much fuss and labelling about it, and it was not until we got out of the town that its particular virtue was apparent. It was the Old Man road, climbing away from the roofs of the houses to the alpine meadows under the grim and beetling heights. A wandering path that took us over rushing becks, under cliffs, into silent spaces of rocks at the foot of the high points, where slim temporary waterfalls tumbled down precipitous rocks. The clouds were touching the summits and a horrid gloom cast satanic shades over those huge, barren lumps of

179

rock. It was no place to live in at all. But it was big and grand. It terrified you, and braced you, and you could scramble about, a tiny pink speck among all that hard formidable strength, and come down into Coniston again with the feeling that you were a size larger for the experience.

Coming down from the Old Man you look over the lake to the gentler shore, the Unter-Walden, as Ruskin called them, and it is on the edge of the woods, near down to the lake, that you see Brantwood, his house. Poor Ruskin, who drove himself mad trying to knock some sense into the heads of the stupid and vulgar Victorians, had sufficient wits left to live out the vague end of his life in loveliness ; for that meadow-land between the woods and the lake, with its view across to Coniston and its great mounts, must be the loveliest place in all Lancashire.

They utter no lie in Coniston, however loudly they proclaim it, when they offer to provide you with tea. Our table was spread with ten items, and wherever you stretched a hand there was something good to clutch, including that curious, sweetly intoxicating rum butter that turns a one-and-sixpenny tea into a Bacchanalia.

A swift medley of bus, rain, Ulverston, rain, cinema, rain, bus, Grange, rain and train brought us back to Arnside. The total effect of the wayward excursion had been to make us want the barrow again, to travel again slowly in our own distinguished fashion, and to wander into the hills away from the tourist routes according to the vagaries of the weather.

XVII

ARNSIDE TO KENDAL

ARNSIDE was charming in the morning. It has great fascination with those wide sands that appear and disappear so quickly, and are washed clean by the tide every day. That morning they seemed infinite in extent as they merged into the mist, a pale, mysterious tract of subtly changing golds and golden greys, fantastically clean and perfect, like virgin snow, in its smooth unbroken forms. There was an innocent feeling in the air in spite of a crazy mix-up of weather, of mist and sun, of showers on the mountains, black clouds overhead, and a rainbow spanning those immense, ethereal sands.

The barrow came out of the shed without reluctance. It had been shoved in casually several evenings ago and had remained safely there, but the farm was deserted and we could find no one to thank for its safe-keeping. We pulled along the hinterland of Arnside, and a gentle shower christened our new departure. It was soon over, the sun became clearer, and the road carried us along by the edge of the sandy estuary. It was delightful; the hills were before us, and innumerable groups of trees and emerald meadows lay over the golden sand, small distant parks and groves, beautifully composed under the blue hills. The wind began to blow and a stirring sky sailed across the heavens.

We hoped that this was the beginning of better days. Obviously the weather was mending, it was " taking oop," as they say there, and we were determined to knock out some stirring life and adventures to make up for the slow, damp times. We were effete with the crawling from shower to shower and being balked of our audiences by the continual rain, and we pushed along recovering spirit and energy with every turn of the wheels. We would be in Kendal before night. In a few days we would cut across the hills and dales to Coniston, and we would travel south to explore the Furness peninsula in this tardy blossoming of the summer.

In the meantime progress was delayed, and before we had cleared Sandside we had three receptions on the road. First it was a large car that drew up after passing us.

" Those people looked at us very hard," said Winifred.

" Everybody does ! They've only stopped to light a cigarette."

" They are backing ! " And instinctively Winifred pushed her hat crooked that was straight, and I shook out a trouser leg.

" Are you the Wilkinsons ? "

The car was full of ladies, one of whom had recognised the barrow from descriptions. The other occupants were visitors from the States, and we blushed for the reputation of the Empire that we did not seem to be upholding at all suitably. We had been caught in the act ; these eccentric activities are safer in the reading than in the actuality.

The second encounter was Mr. Llewellyn, who hospitably offered all the resources of his hostelry, gave useful information as to roads, and cunning advice about the more recherché points of Coniston.

And then it was Mr. Newsham, who had followed us in the books, and who had a camp for us on his farm and a vagrant pitch for the show on the green by the water's edge. The green where the beggar appears regularly every Sunday morning and asks for assistance to reach Barrow, only a few miles away. He either gets too much or too little help, or, as I hope, he goes to Barrow during the week and begs for assistance to get to Sandside. Mr. Newsham is a traveller himself, by car, and we compared notes as to roads. He also had run the gamut of the series of gates across the road in the Trough of Bowland. At the first he said " Thank you " to the gate-opener without adventure ; at the second the same innocent procedure had produced a bit of a stare, but at the third " Thank you " the guardian of the gate had said, " Thank you, hell ! " which, I am afraid, was only too revealing.

The road turned from the estuary and we walked the leafy road to Milnthorpe, crossed the main road to Kendal with extreme care, and wandered round by Ackenthwaite and Woodhouse. The road rose, lifting us above the country, and at last we were free of the petty contemporary life and came out into the universal life of the ages, the world of a wide country and a great sky, of a wind blowing, of all the ravishing form and colour of meadow, plain, and hill. The sun burned through the racing clouds, flashing its light now here, now there, picking out a group of hills, leaving them in blue shadow, and passing on across the landscape in an ever-changing development of subtle colour and silent movement. It was music, it was painting, it was drama all carried out on a wide scene in the living day, and we, walking, using our flesh and blood, feeling the wind, sensing the sun, open to every mysterious influence, were living parts of all that beauty and life.

Before leaving the contemporary life for this poetic outburst we had not neglected to fill the hamper with food, and for the first time for many days we were able to sit in the sun like beggars under a hedge. The leitmotiv of the meal was rum butter, a carton of which we had found in Milnthorpe, and our company a cow and some heifers that looked at us expectantly through the bars of a gate. They were excited by our attentions or the rum butter which they licked up, and the heifers began to butt each other like excited children. Then the cow began to butt the heifers, and it was altogether like a children's party. The farmers should be grateful to us for amusing their bored and lonely stock in the fields. I am convinced that horses, for instance, are always looking for company. Only that morning we came up to a field with a horse looking over the wall expectantly at the road. He pricked his ears when he saw the barrow, and on his side of the wall he stalked along with us on tiptoe with excitement ; at the end of his field, when he could accompany us no farther, he gave us a parting neigh, tossed his head, and careered round the field, galloping and bucking in a frenzy of pleasure. All the animals like to see us on the road; pigs have spoken to us; goats we have often fraternised with; sheep have no social sense, but a cow can stop eating to look at you moodily; dogs are always stirred, and a cock will usually crow at our passing.

The road continued to behave itself, and to provide us with the proper ecstasies. It had a good verge and flowers all the way, particularly the delicate crane's-bill, with hungry butterflies making the most of the fine day dancing in groups over the blue flowers. And it was on this road that we first encountered the wild raspberries that grow so refreshingly on these northern roads. What people we encountered took us naturally. They smiled, told us the way; they were not ashamed to appear kind. By the woods of Levens there was the sound of rushing water in the trees, and we wandered down to the side of Kent Force to stare, fascinated, at the river swirling over the rocks and winding away through the wooded banks. Then it was Sedgewick Hall and the road rising higher, and we came into the Kendal country with Sizergh Castle over among the trees and the long bare hump of Scouts Scar against the sky. Then we were on top of Kendal and all its grey houses clustered in the great green hollow among the hills. This was progress. This was travelling; we just went on and on through the lovely day, and having left the sea in the morning, we were coming into a new world in the evening, to Kendal among the hills.

The puppets did not enter Kendal entirely as strangers. They had been there before to give a winter performance, a rapid visit between two railway journeys, and they were now invited to camp in the orchard of their good friends there. We began asking the way as soon as possible, and very soon had our heads filled with intricate instructions that served, at least, to make an impression of the town. We must pass the factory of those excellent K boots, some of which were on our feet ; we must pass the end of the first bridge, walk along by the river past the piano factory, cross the second bridge, make for Stramongate, go over a third bridge and turn by a church. That is Kendal, a winding river, the grey stone bridges, grey stone houses on the hilly roads, modest factories, ancient street names, and a comfortable density of busy, pleasant people. With frequent inquiries, and in spite of several offers to lead us to the circus, we negotiated the busy streets and drew near to the appointed orchard.

It was then that we grew nervous. Our friends were away, and it would soon be necessary to establish ourselves alone among somebody else's apples and pears. Moreover, we were in a very respectable road, among the villas in fact, and to introduce a tent among those tidy houses and in a villa orchard hardly seemed to be playing the game. Was it cricket ? And, what was more alarming, would a policeman discover us playing at Red Indians in the garden of the unoccupied house ? We were going slowly after twelve miles of walking, and as these questions weighed on our minds we slowed down a little more.

But Kendal is a miraculous place as far as we are concerned. It has a demon which embraces puppets, as you will see. Before us was the house and a letter-box and a tall, handsome man posting a letter. He turned for a moment, glanced at us, hesitated, turned again and walked away. But in that brief moment I had been carried away to Hutton-le-Hole in Yorkshire when tramping in the county years ago. While the puppets had been performing in a garden there a handsome stranger had been discovered looking over the hedge, and was invited to join the audience. This man, posting a letter, was that same mysterious stranger. We had enjoyed a brief encounter at the winter performance, and we now dashed after him, on the strength of this acquaintance, hoping that he would aid and abet us in penetrating the orchard. In the meantime he also had been thinking and turned again, and, better than leading us to the orchard, he took us into his house for tea. He had not known we were coming to Kendal, and it was entirely chance that the letter had been posted at that moment.

Tea ! That was good after twelve miles of tramping and without the trouble of setting the tent ! And so were the chairs, and the company, and we sat back not so very inclined to rush off to the orchard. It was in this breathing space that the bell rang, and our host brought in a lady who had seen the barrow passing through Kendal, and, having just read one of the puppet books, had said to herself, " Can this be IT ? " It was a further surprise to come on us in the room, and, what with one coincidence and another, the puppets received a charming invitation to give a performance. We were going to Wigton, and after that we must return to Kendal.

It was now time for the orchard. The tea had made us lazy, and our legs were beginning to stiffen after the day's walking, which had been long and hilly. There had been a heavy shower, but our handsome friend, who was not going to camp, led us boldly into the precincts, and we were soon left in the orchard, and with the key of the house in case the weather should be impossible. We looked at the cold ground, which was of a sloping nature ; the grass was long, and the shower had made it confoundedly wet. We looked at the greenhouses, the potting shed, and the coal cellar with a vague idea of promoting our comfort, and then we looked at the house, and particularly at a covered stoop, where, finally, we spread the inflated beds. We were going to Wigton the next day, and it was hardly worth while setting the tent until we returned.

A great deal of rain fell while we were at Wigton, and we began to despair about the coming of summer. In fact, things looked very black when we arrived back at Kendal on a wet evening and minus the puppets, which had been mislaid en route. We looked at the orchard again, then at the stoop, and finally opened the french windows into the house and put the inflated beds on the dining-room carpet. Then we worried the railway officials, and in the late evening learned that the puppets had found their way back, but without their theatre. Well, that was reassuring. We could improvise a theatre for the next evening, and we went to bed on the dining-room carpet with a charming view of the chair legs and the feet of the dining-table. I must say, in justice to our absent hosts, that we had been instructed to have the beds made up, but we were shy of disturbing this dust-sheeted house that did not belong to us, and it was more picaresque, at least not exactly bourgeois, to sleep with our heads among the chair legs.

The morning was decidedly wet as we breakfasted in the kitchen, and having been informed that the theatre had also arrived at the station, our minds were freed for further mischief. We opened another room of the house, and discovered books. There were books in the dining-room ; there were books in the hall, and books in the kitchen. But this was a library ; the room was built of books ! They were double deep on the shelves and, as authors ourselves, we stood enthralled at having discovered the man who actually buys books. And they were real books, none of your sixpenny editions.

Naturally, we looked for our own works first. It made me sulky not to find mine, and Winifred much too elated to find hers. From that moment we had no further conversation, not from jealousy, but because we had each retired to a chair with half a dozen volumes each. It was not for hours that we looked up and realised that we were in Kendal and that there were preparations to be made for the evening performance.

It was Saturday morning, and market day in Kendal, with the streets crowded with the farmers in from the dales. Everybody carried at least one basket, and many three or four. You had to steer your way round the baskets or they got you in the ribs, or in the small of the back. I suppose it all becomes instinctive in time, and you subconsciously allow for the extra girth of the passer-by occasioned by the panniers. We enjoyed it. Baskets are good craft work, and to find a real market, personally served by real farmers with fresh local produce, is, in these days, a sacred experience.

A whiskered old gentleman from the middle of the last century, and plainly in town for the day, directed us to the Butter Market. His eyes were clear and blue, and his rounded cheeks a brilliant boyish red. His clean, hardy appearance promoted the idea that any human being ought to look just like this before you took their works or thoughts seriously. It was the proper machinery for the human spirit to work in. His soft speech, inherent with natural culture, directed us with a warm smile. He was eager that we should find the market—that we should have everything we wanted. Unfortunately the books had retarded us, and the Butter Market was emptying, but in the large hall there were still some white cloths on the trestle tables, some flowers, and numbers of those flat, oblong, scrubbed wooden boxes with brass hinges in which the precious and beautifully made butter is carried. It was remarkable to find so much hand-made butter in these days of international yellow grease, and for it to be sold among flowers, on white cloths, was to turn the market into an Arts and Crafts exhibition.

But Kendal, of course, is a distinguished town. A local bookshop is always a good gauge to the mentality of a district, and there are many larger towns that cannot show such an interesting, selective, and modern stock of reading as you will find in Roberts's shop in Kendal. It would be interesting to trace the exact influence of the Society of Friends here. All this district of northern Lancashire and the Westmorland border was travelled by George Fox himself; the town has always had a large meeting and a school too, in the days when Friends were pioneers in education, and it is more than a suspicion that the Society has helped to make a background for that bookshop.

Kendal is an ancient settlement with more cultures in it than just the contemporary. It has a castle on a green hill outside the town, and its woollen industry goes back to the fourteenth century. It is not limited to one industry or to abnormal mobs of one kind of work-people, and it is surrounded by a country of small farmers who have been worn by Time and Nature into a refined and gentle race. It is on the edge of the hills and the lonely fells, and by its geographical position must have been cut off from a good deal of mob influence. One imagines that it has a mind of its own. Its central road bears a great weight of traffic, but it looks like a passing traffic, a foreign invasion that has not yet affected to any great extent this old grey town in the hollow of the green hills.

We looked at Kendal, and we prepared the puppets, but it was not at all certain how many people would come to the performance. The show had been arranged very hastily, and we were prepared for a small friendly group, but at the hour for starting the hall was full, the yard outside was packed with cars, and still more people were approaching the door. They were pushed in somewhere by the cruel but efficient stewards, and the puppets did their best, in the midst of a vagabondage, to rise to the responsibilities of the occasion, responsibilities which included his worship the mayor. There was no doubt about the audience ; we have seldom met a better. They threw a good deal at us, but only in the shape of applause, and it was quite obvious that the people of Kendal have very good taste. They liked the puppets ; there is little more to be said.

With all this we were getting a trifle jaded. A regular life is always advocated by the exponents of health culture, and you could not say that walking, camping, travelling by train, performing in Wigton, examining Carlisle on the way, losing the puppets, and sleeping on a dining-room carpet was exactly a regular life. It was late when we got back to the house, and rest was imperative. The orchard and the stoop were ignored ; we considered the dining-room floor, cast a calculating eye over the padded chairs and the table-cover, considered the rugs in the hall and the umbrella stand, and finally, under the decadent influence of the house, we ascended the stairs and commandeered a couple of good beds for the night.

XVIII

WHAT A BLOW

WATER had been pouring over England for more than two months. It was going to ridiculous lengths, and so were the plants in the gardens. The rain had begun in May, it was now August, still raining, and you could see no sign of it doing anything else. It was a very quiet and respectable business. Not much thunder and lightning. Nothing fussy, in fact. It was only that nearly every day the low, loose clouds just sprinkled water quietly over the earth in large, loose drops and calmly devastated outdoor activities, the sort of activities that we were interested in.

We wanted to get out of Kendal, but the Monday morning was so wet that we put off the start to the afternoon. A friend was to drive us over that formidable hill, Scouts Scar, into Underbarrow, where we would get out the tent and camp again, but as we watched the sheets of rain drifting over the grey walls and green fields of Kendal we thought it better to sit among the books and wait for a drier moment. It was irritating. We had risen early and packed, and with our imaginations screwed up to the point of camping again in a new country it was impossible to think of anything else. We read with one eye on the book and one on the weather, and neither book nor weather was satisfactory. I was finishing off a life of Ruskin, reading of how he travelled with a specially designed coach, a courier and a valet. It was preposterous, but rather consoling, too. It must have been so troublesome and humiliating to travel with a couple of servants always hanging round, interfering with everything, and never allowing one to boil an egg for oneself or to have any fun at all.

By the afternoon a break had come in the rain. The car arrived and we began to pack, and by the time we had carried the packages out to the road and had them piled unprotected on the pathway, a positive cloudburst descended. We sat patiently in the car, waiting, watching the water dribbling over our property, but it seemed that we were waiting for nothing at all. The rain continued maliciously and we carried the gear back to the house. Our friend would take us out to look at Underbarrow and we would come back to the house for the night. To-morrow we could act according to the conditions.

We cannot have gone far before the rain ceased ; at all events, immediately we were over the Scar we were looking down on Underbarrow, radiant in the sunlight, a ravishing scene of this green valley, backed by the very blue mountains. We crossed to the lower hills on the other side of the valley to a whitewashed farm, and it was all so inviting, and the clouds were blowing away so rapidly, that we mounted the car again, went back to Kendal, and returned with the barrow and everything. We put the tent in a high field because of foolish notions about views, and spread our inflated beds in their right place. If the evening continued to clear, instead of having our heads among the table legs this night they would be among the stars.

It was glorious. We were able to breakfast in the open and to potter easily about the tent. It was not a positively healthy summer day, but it would do. The sky was high, but wild, and the air was not only warm but uncomfortably enervating as well. But it all looked lovely. From the tent we looked under a dark tree down to the bright alluvial plain lying between the hills, a green draught-board of flat fields with dark patches of peat-moss. And at the end of it, less than ten miles away, was the slim end of Morecambe Bay and the quarry at Sandside, a tiny gleaming vision as seen through the wrong end of a glass. Scouts Scar was across the valley, a huge barrier cutting out Kendal, and Shap, and all that country, a long grey cliff rising from a sea of fields and woods that climbed nearly up to its ridge. On our side of the valley were the smaller hills of bracken and pasture, breaking into rocky little summits—the " rough lots " the farmers called them, and kept a few chickens and sheep on them, cut the bracken for bedding, and collected pailfuls of " blackbums " from the brambles growing over the stone walls.

But the rough lots were built for poets and artists more than for farmers. There were many things we ought to have been doing that morning, but a rising path over a stone stile caught our fancy, and, following it, we were led on to be fascinated by the way it disappeared into thick bracken. Pushing through the bracken we could feel the path underfoot, and presently it came into sight again, across some short, springy turf, diving again into bracken and emerging again to get round some protruding rocks. It was delightful, this game of hide-and-seek with a wandering path that evaded us in the end, and we found our own rather damp way across a bog and up a miniature Everest. All this had carried us considerably higher in the world, and we could now see all the Lake District, except the lakes, the towns and the houses or the poets—well, we could see the mountain-tops—and all Underbarrow and the green and verdant valley running down to Sandside.

It is a backwater of England. There is no money in it, hardly what you would call a village, and no town. Its roads are ways of fruit and flowers, and in its winding lanes, among the riot of ferns and brackens, grow the raspberry and blackberry beneath the nut bushes. It seems to have missed all progress except for a radio or two and a wandering bus, and the farmers still use horse-drawn carts. Consequently it is one of the most beautiful places in England, and from its fields and small farms and orchards emanates a green serenity and the tranquillity of sane and honest human living.

After an idle day, if any hours lived in that valley could be called idle, we came down into the farmyard with the puppets, and began setting up the theatre outside the house. There was to be a show when work was done, and as we put up the booth some of that work was going on round us. It was feeding-time, or nearly, and an extraordinary family had gathered in the yard, all clamouring in a variety of noises for food. The cows in the shippon had been milked, and lowed gently, but the very young calves, incarcerated behind stone walls, were letting off like lusty foghorns. Five kittens attempted to play, but they too had smelt milk, and from time to time opened minute pink mouths and asked for it ; or tried to crawl under the gate to the dairy ; or did get under and were chased out by stamping wooden clogs. Chickens were waiting for maize, and ducks demanding meal, while geese were stalking backwards and forwards, heads in air, screeching haughtily to be attended to. Two enormous sows, one with a litter of eight, snuffed and grunted and cocked little greedy eyes in the direction of the house. All the time wooden clogs were beating a tattoo on the flags inside the gate ; the milk was being separated and strained into various buckets, making seductive sounds that set all the mouths watering in this animal parade assembled outside the gate. Now the gate opens, and Tom Carruthers, in blue linen coat and white of hair, comes out with a couple of pails of meal and milk for the calves. As he walks across the yard and down to the stalls the whole comic family of agitated animals stalks after him. It is as good as a puppet-show to us, especially when the sows are busy in their trough and one goose and several chickens peck cheekily between their legs and under their fat chaps.

When all this quacking, mooing, screeching family had been stowed away for the night, the pails wiped clean and the flags brushed down, chairs and forms were brought out to the grass and rock at the front of the house and set before the theatre. An audience of about a dozen took their places, made up from the house and the neighbours, and the puppets proceeded with their stuff. Local allusions were warmly approved of, and the performance was helped greatly owing to there being a real Martha in the audience as well as a puppet Martha in the theatre. This seemed to affect the boys strangely. Queer noises came from them at odd moments, and I suppose they were in that state of nature when the Christian name of an elderly lady seems excruciatingly funny. They were afraid to laugh at the right time, but held themselves in, shaking with suppressed laughter, until it escaped forcibly in a series of explosions.

There were unexpected additions to the programme. At the first blast of the squeaky music there came from over the orchard gate a loud challenge from one of the haughty geese, and he did not cease from challenging and marching up and down before the gate at every musical interlude. The kittens got into the theatre and played with the properties among my feet, dragging some of them out into view of the audience, and the sight of a very small kitten gambolling with a black bottle was very well received. And one of the delightful kittens allowed the puppets to lift it on the stage, where it stayed and played with them as well as any Toby. A nice, friendly show in the farmyard, and we collected a delicious loaf of light, wheaty, home-made bread and some real freshly made English butter—a good night's work.

We could not tear ourselves away from Underbarrow. A heavenly day came out of nowhere, and again we were deceived into thinking that summer was on the way. Instead of tearing off to somewhere not quite so good, we stayed where we were to enjoy the luxury of being able to loiter about this lovely farm in the hills. I had known it as a small boy many years ago, and it had left an indelible impression on my mind. Coming to it from the restrictions of a small house in a small town, life had suddenly expanded into a great affair with some meaning in it, and to play at feeding calves and chickens, at hay-making, at harvesting, with the oats being cut with scythes, and to be able to scamper about the irregular hilly yard, the barns and sheds and cow houses, to fire off guns which knocked me over and missed the rabbits, was one breathless excitement after another.

And the food ! nearly all of which was of the district. The home-made bread seemed like cake, and the butter was an ephemeral charm in the mouth. Wonderful baskets were brought into the harvest fields by the girls at " drinking " time, baskets packed with the delectable bread and butter, apple pasties, and damson pasties, and cake, wrapped in snowy white linen, while the " drinking " part was tea in a large can. There were oddments in the way of blackberry jelly, raspberry vinegar, a cough cure—compounded of oatmeal, butter, and brown sugar—that used to give me a cough, it seemed so good, and then there were the rice puddings with rum in them. An early acquaintance with these artistic productions has given me only a fierce scorn for the ingenuous and naïve belief in great, centralised productions of factory food.

And now here was this farm, as near as possible exactly as it was all those years ago. There was a machine for cutting the grass, some bicycles about, a wireless receiver, some new furniture, and the old trout in the spring under the stone slab is dead. They are small changes and the lovely hummocky fields, the beehives in the pretty stone-walled and terraced garden, the plum tree against the end of the house, the many damson trees, and the smell of peat smoke are all still there. And still, every Saturday, the farm cart is packed with eggs, with the traditional butter box, with flowers and any vegetables that are going, the horse harnessed, and away they trot over the great Scouts Scar, down into Kendal. The horse is considered better for the hills than a car—but that is probably only an escapist excuse or perhaps it just happens that the horse is more economical in the circumstances.

As the farm, so all the countryside, and to walk as we did to Scouts Scar was to pass by marvellous grassy ways among the crane's-bill and the raspberries, down by the water-mill and the clear beck in the grass, and up the road to the whitewashed inn, the Punch Bowle, under walls hanging with ferns, by other small farms, and finally to mount that high, bleak scar perched above the Lake country, revealing the wild, tossed-up ranges that rise above the hidden lakes. It revealed some queer clouds too, low down on the horizon, and we came back to the farm with a subtle change creeping into the air like an invisible blight.

The farm kitchen was warm, and the peat fire, with a chirping cricket in its depths, sent out a drowsy incense. The same cricket had been chirping there when I was a small boy, and now, as then, flowers were being made into bunches for the market, large bunches of fine sweet-peas, to be sold for only tuppence the bunch. And then, all those years ago, I had sat fascinated by the Westmorland talk that went on over my head; long, long tales and discussions, carried on in the deep voices of men drowsy with work in the fields, and not one word of which I could understand; but it was none the less fascinating for all that. Now the London Symphony Orchestra played, and the Westmorland language was surprisingly easy to understand—a soft, pleasantly turned speech, full of colour and music, and very refined. They spoke of selling flowers in the market, of how customers count the stalks before parting with their pennies, and of an old well-to-do couple who would buy a dozen bunches cheap and then hawk them again at the full price. It is a wonderful year for peas, and the oats are doing well; the wool is fetching better prices, and damsons are promising. You never heard such sanguine farmers, sitting round the peat fire with the cheerful cricket chirping incessantly.

When we went out the sky was overcast, and it was heavy work walking up the road, climbing over the gate and dragging up the hilly meadow to the tent. We were going to move in the morning, down the valley over the border into Lancashire again, but our spirits sank in this heavy atmosphere that had all the feeling of more rain. More rain! It was too absurd, and getting into the sleeping-bags we protested against this summer, the most rainy for forty years.

" If it rains to-morrow, I'm going home," I said.

" I'm already packing," said Winifred.

" It's such a waste of time, this hanging about in the wet weather. Can't work, or do anything properly."

" No, nor play, either. It's no fun."

" We're a cricket match that can't be played."

Quite suddenly a low, deafening roar filled our ears. It was the rain, extraordinarily heavy, thundering on the tent.

" Listen to that ! It's the worst yet."

" I wish we hadn't pitched on this very exposed place."

" Just listen to it—the tent will be squashed flat."

" It sounds like another week of it. We ought to have put this tent on a raft from the beginning."

" I wish we had pitched in a more sheltered place. If there's any wind it will be awkward."

As if in mockery a long-drawn sigh came from the tree below the tent. It died away, and then, from somewhere higher in the hills, came a distant, melancholy wail. The steady rain roared and pressed on the tent.

" There was a gale warning in the news," said Winifred.

" Yes, but we've had so much bad weather that I took no notice of it."

" Well, it's some consolation to know that the storms have increased in splendour as we've gone on."

" It was pretty bad at Edale."

" Yes, but it was quite mild when I joined you at Wigan."

" It was more showery round Preston ; we did get some thunder there."

" And then Blackburn ; it was heavier rain there."

" Bowland was an improvement on Blackburn— more among the hills, I suppose."

" That was a good one at Yealand. The rain was heavier and the thunder and lightning quite good."

" Arnside only produced a mere drizzle, comparatively speaking."

" There was one very excellent night at Kendal. I thought the house was coming down."

" Well, this sounds like the grand finale."

By this time the wind had settled down to give us a good battering. It was a nasty wind. It was like an irritated monster, snatching and tugging at the tent out of the darkness. It was one of those nights that does not succeed in dividing two days, and I lay awake ready at any moment to rush out and replace torn-up tent pegs. The gusts of the gale tore into the tree, roared through its branches, pounced down on us in the tent, shook us for a wild and sportive moment, and shrieked off in triumph into the hills. When the first dismal light crept through the rain there was the added fascination of watching the tent being jerked now this way, now that, and to see the poles bending at times like pieces of soap.

I dressed and after a time awakened Winifred, who is a talented sleeper.

" Sounds a bit gusty," she remarked indifferently. And then, instinctively, with a " Good Lord," she had leapt up and dressed before she was properly awake.

It was exactly the right moment. The tent was caught in a flurry, swayed for a moment, and then, with the wheezy sound of splintering cane, gracefully subsided on our heads. The front pole had broken and was sticking through the tent roof and the fly-sheet. Rigging the tent loosely on the shortened pole and supporting the bulging cotton on my shoulders, we contrived to make sufficient space to gather up our tackle into the boxes. And I lit the primus and made some coffee. Not content with that, while I still supported the tent, Winifred made some toast.

"We are going home," we said with one voice. "The weather conditions of late have been far from in keeping with what would naturally be expected in July."